...ccording to Mack Hanan, "There ...one rule for increasing profits on ...les: Concentrate on penetrating ...ur key accounts . . . . Key ...ccount selling strategies can grow ...ur business because they grow ...e businesses of your principal ...ustomers."

The first edition of *Key Account Selling* pioneered a sales approach ...hat quickly proved its success and ...ecame the standard game plan in ...ales. This new edition shows how ...he key account concept has ...volved and how smart salespeople ...an adapt.

No longer are key accounts nec- ...essarily the biggest, most frequent, ...or most loyal customers. They are ...the ones that are *growing* and that ...help their suppliers *grow*. In *Key Account Selling, Second Edition*, Mack Hanan spells out the new strategies needed to reach them, with hard-hitting guidance on how ...to:

❑ Target customers with the high- est growth potential

❑ Reach those customers at the top tier and work with them as part- ners

❑ Use a database to find high-mar- gin opportunities

❑ Devise account plans that will turn those opportunities into sales

❑ Prove added value that ensures repeat sales

Your selection of customers that you can help grow — in the most certain ways and in the shortest periods of time — is the single most important decision you can make. It must come first because it will determine *every* other decision you make: what your product lines should consist of; what services you must offer to support them; what values you must deliver; who your decision makers will be in customer organizations; what kinds of sales force you should recruit . . . every- thing.

Key account selling goes no- where if you make the wrong selec- tions. If you choose customers you cannot grow, they will be unable to grow you. But if you choose cor- rectly, you will have discovered your "growth engine." The strate- gies in this book will make certain that you drive it profitably.

Mack Hanan is an international consultant on all aspects of business growth. His firm, The Wellspring Group, works with *Fortune* 500 companies in the U.S., Europe, and the Far East. He is the author of a number of AMACOM books, includ- ing *Consultative Selling* and *Outper- formers.*

# *KEY ACCOUNT SELLING*

## Second Edition

Other AMACOM books by Mack Hanan that support the strategies of Key Account Selling are:

*Successful Market Penetration: How to Shorten the Sales Cycle by Making the First Sale the First Time*

*Customer Satisfaction: How to Maximize, Measure, and Market Your Company's "Ultimate Product"*

# KEY ACCOUNT SELLING

## Second Edition

## *MACK HANAN*

90-2449

# amacom

## AMERICAN MANAGEMENT ASSOCIATION

This book is available at a special
discount when ordered in bulk quantities.
For information, contact Special Sales Department,
AMACOM, a division of American Management Association,
135 West 50th Street, New York, NY 10020.

Library of Congress Cataloging-in-Publication Data

Hanan, Mack.
    Key account selling / Mack Hanan.—2nd ed.
        p.    cm.
    Includes index.
    ISBN 0-8144-5985-4
    1. Selling—Key accounts.  I. Title.
HF5438.8.K48H36  1989
658.8'105—dc20                    89-6728
                                         CIP

Printing number

10 9 8 7 6 5 4 3 2

To **Paula Brown,**

who used these strategies
to help AT&T take its first steps
from monolithic utility to
competitive enterprise
by installing millions of new
profit dollars in her
key customer accounts
and, as a result, in AT&T as well

# Preface to the Second Edition

When the first edition of this book was written, it was fashionable to "sell something to everybody," moving volume and bumping up market share as much as possible without too much regard for who was doing the buying. All sales were good sales, money was money, and what difference did it really make where the profits came from as long as they kept coming? Even then, though, it could be seen how false a premise for success this kind of thinking could be.

Something called the quality of profits was beginning to be considered along with their quantity. How rich were they in terms of margin per unit of sale? How rewarding were they compared to the investment required to make them? Continuity of profit making also became an issue. Did the first sale lead to additional sales without incurring the same start-up costs of penetration over and over again? Did a customer offer progressive migration opportunities, or was the first sale likely to be the only sale and therefore the last sale? A third consideration focused on a customer company's own sales. Was the company growing its markets? If not, where would it earn the funds to buy?

Such questions took sales and marketing managers away from their laundry lists of product features and benefits and required them to look critically, some of them for the first time, at their customers. Where should the sales force be concentrating its resources? Who would provide the biggest bang for the buck, that is, the greatest return-on-investment? Of all the potential customers in a market, who would offer a growing, long-term demand base that would justify extra attention? Customers who qualified after this kind of examination qualified themselves as key accounts.

For most managers, defining key accounts seemed simple. They were the consistently heavy users, customers who bought in volume on a dependable basis and who had demonstrated loyalty—and paid promptly—over the years. Customers like these were regarded as the foundation of the business, the bedrock of a supplier's growth. Managers who wore lapel buttons that said "I Love Sales" sometimes added in parentheses "That I Can Count On." Sales they could count on represented money in the bank before each year began. Many sales representatives were halfway to quota on January 2.

Curiosity, and some vague unease, prompted some managers to look more deeply. Were the biggest customers the best? Were volume sales the most profitable? How sustainable did margins prove to be in selling to major customers? How many extra services thrown in "free" to keep the customer were actually detracting from profits? Questions like these revealed new truths. An inverse relationship between volume and profits was frequently discovered. Costs of sales were found to nullify earnings. Major customers were quite often stable businesses, not growing, and while their order levels were reliably high they provided no growth impetus to their sources of supply.

As a result, managers on the leading edges of their industries started to conceive of a new notion of what a key account really was. It had to be a customer who could "grow" them, that is—an ongoing source of profits, preferably a rising one, whose own growth would drive the growth of its suppliers. The best accounts would be customers that were growing steadily, the faster the better, and whose prospects for future growth were soundly based in the growth of the markets they served. Customers who were growing would be golden, but never easy to come by. Did you have to be lucky to do business with them?

Managers who believed that luck was the residue of design set about to create strategies that, if they could not guarantee a supply of growing customers who would be key to them, could as least increase the possibility of a constant and sufficient number of customers growing rapidly enough to grow their suppliers. These managers developed a new definition of a key account: a customer that they can help to grow.

Key account sales strategies can grow your business because they can grow the businesses of your principal customers. They are growth strategies. They transform the sales process from an exchange of goods and services for money to an exchange of growth values. As a supplier, you trade your ability to improve customers' profits—the profits that source their growth—for the customers' ability to improve your own profits. You provide improvement for them by reducing some of their significant costs or helping them to increase their revenues and earnings through new sales to their own customers. They provide improvement for you by rewarding what you do for them with higher margins based on your value. They also help you lower your costs of selling to them by condensing your sales cycle and freeing you as a rule from the expenses of competitive bidding.

Selecting customers that you can help grow the most, most dependably, and in the shortest periods of time is your single most important decision. It must be given top priority because it will determine every other decision you make: what your product lines should consist of, what services you must offer to support them, what values you must deliver from your products and services, who your principal decision makers will be in customer organizations, what kind of sales force you should recruit to deal at these customer levels most effectively—in short, everything.

Key account selling starts with the selection of your key accounts. It goes nowhere if you make the wrong selections. If you choose customers you cannot grow, they will be unable to grow you. If you choose correctly, however, you will discover your growth engine. The strategies in this book will make certain that you drive the engine profitably.

# Contents

xi

# KEY
# ACCOUNT
# SELLING

## Second Edition

# Introduction

Two strategies will make or break profits through the year 2000.

One is to structure a sales force along key account lines to concentrate personal selling. Key accounts are the 20 percent of all customers that contribute up to 80 percent of the profits. These "20 percenters" are every seller's major sources of revenues and earnings. The second strategy is to concentrate sales to your accounts at their top tier of decision makers, the middle and upper managers who control a customer's profit centers and cost centers.

In an increasing number of industries, the mass sale of products on a price-performance basis has become obsolete as a major profit source. The combination of increasing sales costs and shrinking margins has made selling to the bottom-tier customers progressively more cost-ineffective. Sellers can no longer afford complete market coverage with complete product lines, selling tonnage or gallonage to anyone and everyone, even at break-even prices. The sales function can no longer

1

afford to work for the manufacturing process. Nor can the sales function continue to subsidize platoons of vendor sales representatives who practice ill-named "professional selling skills" in an attempt to establish distinctions without a difference between their commodity-type offerings and the virtually identical commodity offerings of direct competitors.

Bottom-tier selling is price selling. It is high-cost, low-margin selling. It is adversary selling, pitting the aggressive persuasiveness of self-seeking product differentiators against the self-seeking defensiveness of purchasers. Only one can win—at least until the next time. Approximately 80 percent of most companies' sales volume takes place in this basement tier of the sales process. Yet it accounts for only 20 percent or less of all profits.

The upper tier is another world. Here the percentages are reversed. For this reason, it is the only customer tier where direct selling pays off. For all other sales— sales made to the 80 percent of customers in the bottom tier—everything must be done to shift the cost burden to a third partner or such indirect strategies as telemarketing or mail order.

Top-tier concentration pays off only if sellers concentrate on managers above the purchasing function— the line-of-business managers who run a customer's profit centers and the business function managers who run cost centers. At these levels, only value-based selling makes sense. Products, services, or systems are irrelevant in themselves. They are relevant only in terms of the dollar value of their bottom-line impact on a customer's business. The asking price can be directly correlated with the customer's added value, enabling margins to be high when customer value is high. Sellers and buyers can consult on how the values can be implemented. They can share their mutual knowledge of the customer's business problems that they can solve together. Both can seek a common objective: to improve customer profits.

In the 1990–2000 time frame, growth (to say nothing of survival) will depend on how well businesses in every industry can manage the 20 percent of their sales resources that contribute up to 80 percent of their profits—their top-tier key account sales forces. Companies that continue to play the two-tier game by universally applying the vendor selling tactics of the bottom tier will perish.

Throughout the past generation, my clients and I have concentrated on top-tier selling as a major corporate growth strategy. We have studied and popularized the two-tier concept. We have advocated the creation of a doctrine for key account selling that is separate and distinct from vendor selling. We have counseled the establishment of a separate sales force that is deliberately recruited, trained, and managed to execute the doctrine. We have given the name Consultative Selling™ to our doctrine. We have written the book on it. Today, thousands of key account sales representatives in hundreds of companies in dozens of industries go by the book. They position themselves in a consultative capacity with high-level decision makers in key accounts. They receive consistently high margins in return for improving customer profits. They crack accounts long denied to their companies—in one case, for as long as half a century. They condense their sales cycles dramatically from 12 months or longer down to 90 to 120 days—sometimes to only a matter of hours. They make their competitors noncompetitive.

™Consultative Selling is a registered trademark of Mack Hanan.

These trained consultative sales representatives regularly demolish competitors who try to neutralize them with traditional vendor selling skills. When they have technically superior products and sell them in a consultative, profit-improving manner, victory is assured. Even when they have only parity products, they almost always prevail. But neither of these conditions is the acid test. What has been the result when their products are technically surpassed by competition? Whenever they are able to demonstrate a superior profit for the customer or even a similar profit that is quicker in coming on stream or is surer, Consultative Selling gives them the crucial advantage.

Sometimes we have been surprised at these results, which defy vendor logic. Sometimes, too, the consultative representatives who make the sales have admitted their own surprise. But customers have not been surprised. They know what their needs are. They know that they must acquire profit, not products. What benefit, they ask, is a supplier's technical superiority unless it can be translated into customer profit superiority? We don't want your technology, they say. That is your cost. We want its impact on our business. That is our profit.

Our doctrine of Consultative Selling has evolved, as all doctrines must, through practical application. We have taught the skills, monitored their implementation, and audited the outcomes. If there were a Latin proverb to synthesize what we have done, it would be "From many experiences, one expertise."

At the leading edge of what we have learned is that Consultative Selling skills are one-third of a comprehensive key account penetration system. Two supportive strategies bracket it on either side. The first is an industry-dedicated key account database. The second strategy is a key account planning process on an account-by-account basis, treating each major customer as an individual market.

The database feeds the account penetration planning process, acting like a warehouse of information about customer problems and opportunities. In turn, the account plan is the staging area for developing proposals to improve customer profits by solving the problems in the database and seizing their opportunities.

This process becomes increasingly selective as it moves from data to plan to proposal. Not all the data in the database will end up in the plan. Only 20 percent or so of a customer's problems and opportunities will be mutually profitable enough to merit consideration during the planning process. Similarly, the profit improvement projects that make it through to the plan will have to be ranked in a priority order of significance and probability. Significance tells the amount of profits that are likely for both you and your customer. Probability tells the likelihood of realizing them.

Consultative Selling, customer databasing, and an account penetration planning process—these are the three interlocking components of our key account system.

In order to make our key account system work, you will have to know how to sell at high margins. You will have to know how to use a database to find high-margin opportunities and how to make an account plan that can be used to turn them into sales. Then you will be able to give the same answer as did Paula Brown, to whom this book is dedicated, to the question "How do you sell so many products?" Her answer was "By never selling the product."

# 1

# Concentration and Dedication

There is one rule for increasing profits on sales: Concentrate on penetrating your key accounts. If less than 80 percent of your management time and talent, your sales planning, your operational funding, and your coaching and counseling is being dedicated to growing your key account business—both existing and prospects—you are not concentrating.

If you have not been concentrating, you have been in good company—good, that is, in terms of major corporations in mainstream industries. For the most part, the *Fortune* 500 has favored a monolithic sales strategy. Every sales representative calls on some key accounts. Every product is sold on price and performance, whether the customer is a key account or not. This is called professional selling. Because it is essentially price selling, there is very little that is professional about it. There is also very little that is unusually profitable.

The heyday of monolithic sales organizations is over. The costs of volume—of making it, warehousing it, selling it, and doing all the paperwork it requires, including collecting on it—have outrun the profits. Cost inflation is one pincer of the profit squeeze. The other is price erosion. As costs go up and prices go down under standardized, homogenized competition, sales proceeds often contribute more to manufacturing costs than profit. Sales support manufacturing instead of the other way around.

There is a place for price-performance selling, or vendor selling: at the purchasing function level, whatever it may be named in your industry. This is the level that issues requests for proposals and invites bids whose sole significant deviation from each other will most likely be in price. If you have mature products, services, or systems whose performance is more or less replicated by competition, they should be vended as commodities in the least costly manner. These transactions flow across the basement tier of a two-tier sales environment.

To earn unusual profits, you must penetrate the top tier of your key accounts. That is where the profits are. In most cases, they are underexploited. It is safe to say that whatever your current profits from key account sales may amount to, they are probably undervalued by one-third to two-thirds of their potential. If this estimate seems high, reduce it by half. If it still seems high, halve it further. It still represents a formidable opportunity, the equivalent of developing a new growth market. Yet it offers far fewer risks than a new market and far more cost-effective rewards.

The risk-reward ratio of key account selling is so unusually favorable because of one unique attribute. A key account is a customer whose profits you can improve significantly through the premium value delivered by what you sell; at the same time your own profits are significantly improved by the premium price you can receive in return. As a result, key account customers want you to sell to them whenever you can demonstrate your ability to improve their profits. If you do not fully capitalize on your sales opportunity, you deprive the customer of added profits. In key account selling, customer sales insistence takes the place of sales resistance.

No less risky strategy for profit growth exists than key account concentration. No greater opportunity to profit from sales exists than maximizing top-tier penetration. Nor is there a business growth strategy that is more certain or more capable of quick payoff.

## Knowing the Customer's Business

Key account selling must take place at a customer's top-tier of business managers. The top-tier is immune to vendor tactics. It is unresponsive to feature and benefit comparisons. It stares glassy-eyed at laundry lists of ingredients, components, formulas, subsystems, process variations, or warranties. It ignores price as a reason to buy, resists the bait of a trial close, and does not take kindly to having its objections overcome. From its perspective, professional selling is amateurish selling. The top-tier deals with vendors simply by declining to deal with them.

Suppliers that do not respect two-tier selling always ask how they can "sell up": "How can we get our sales representatives to stand before a top-level decision maker?" This is the wrong question. Any vendor may make it to the top once. The right question is "How can we get invited back a second time?" Unless that happens, no new knowledge of the customer's business will flow. No decisions to buy will flow either.

How can your key account representatives be invited back? There is only one way. On their first call, they must present new knowledge about improving the customer's business—not knowledge of the representatives' business, not product or process knowledge, not knowledge of your latest terms, conditions, or deals but knowledge of the customer's own business. This is the crucial difference between top-tier and bottom-tier selling. The bottom-tier is paid to hear about your business. The top-tier is paid to learn more about its own.

Concentrating on key account penetration inescapably means concentrating on knowing what the customer's top-tier knows—the businesses of your key accounts. It means knowing customer problems and the dollar values of those problems. It means knowing customer opportunities and the dollar values of those opportunities. It means knowing how you can help solve the problems and help achieve the opportunities. It means knowing the dollar values of your solutions. It means bringing this information into your business in the form of a key account database and positioning the database as the foundation of your key account penetration.

Key account selling is information-intensive. To say the same thing in another way, it is data-dependent. In order to "have the goods" in key account salesmanship, it is not enough to have the product. You must have the customer knowledge that will let you know what financial impact that product will make on a customer's business. The dimensions of this added dollar value are the sum and substance of the dialogues your key account representatives must have with high-level customer decision makers. Otherwise, they will be talking to themselves about themselves, an audience of one and a market of none.

## Managing From Customer Data

The decision to concentrate on key account selling as the bull's-eye of your sales management is, first of all, a decision to manage from a base of customer data, not products. It puts you in the information business. It acknowledges your recognition of the central fact about top-tier selling. For both seller and buyer, information makes up 90 percent of every transaction. Nothing moves until the information moves.

Knowledge of how to improve their businesses is the principal element in any sale to key account customers. Nothing, including your physical ironware, is as important for them as that. When you talk about your products, you may think you are discussing tangibles if they have weight, size and shape, texture, color, or aroma. But these are simple bits and pieces of information. They become important only when you can connect them to the reality of the customer's business by showing the financial values they will deliver. In this way of looking at things, only financial values, not products, are tangible.

As manager of this type of information-transfer business, you will preside over a structure to organize customer data, a method to bring new data into the structure, and a system to let your key account sales force gain access to the data. You will have to store customer data by the divisions or departments you sell to, by the functions within them, and by the individual problems and opportunities within the functions. You will also have to store your solutions to each problem and opportunity, expressed both as product and service systems and in terms of their financial effect on the customer's business. By using your database to mix and match your solutions with customer problems, your key account representatives can come up with the optimal solution based on improved profit for both you and their accounts.

Key account sales representatives working from their databases are the nucleus of your inside top-tier sales team. When they go outside to sell, the sales representatives may be supported by technical, service, financial, and other resource people who will implement their solution on the customer's premises. But at home—and this can be literally at the sales representatives' own homes if they are equipped with portable microcomputers—they and their databases can control each key account by the amount of improved profits they propose for it every year.

## Operating as a Financial Service Business

When you decide to concentrate on the penetration of your key account business opportunity, you give up the traditional positioning of your business. If you currently define the nature of your business in product terms, you will lose it. If the definition of your business is based on its raw materials or its processes, you will lose it, too. So it will be with any definition that has to do with your own business instead of its relationship to the businesses of your key accounts. From the customer's perspective, which must now become your own, your business is a financial service business whose product is improved customer profit.

Financial service businesses are information businesses. They are businesses that deal with information about monetary values. They are personal service businesses that act as stewards of their customers' financial well-being. They consult on the most cost-effective strategies for appreciating each customer's current worth. They are evaluated by results that appear in black and white on the customer's bottom line. Were profits improved? Were they improved as much as promised? Could they have been improved even more? Could they have been improved even faster? Will they continue to be improved? Can someone else improve them more?

Your key account representatives must position themselves as financial service representatives. This does not mean they sell a financial service. It means they provide one. The name of the service is improved profitability for their customers. If your business has a strong product heritage, it may be initially difficult for your representatives to reposition their offerings from hardware to hard dollars; from something that goes into a customer's business to something that comes out of its improved operation; from something that is mature and a commodity to something that is always fresh and welcome—and often all too rare.

If you are in the electronic data processing (EDP) business, your representatives will have to learn how to sell the improved profits resulting from solving a customer's problems through data processing rather than from vending an EDP system itself.

If you are a materials cleaning machinery manufacturer, your representatives will have to learn how to sell the improved profits resulting from solving a customer's problems through materials cleaning rather than from vending cleaning equipment itself.

If you are a food processor, they will have to learn how to sell the improved profits resulting from solving a retailer's problems through stocking your products rather than from vending the products themselves.

Even if you are a stockbroker, a banker, or an insurer—a true financial service professional—your representatives will have to learn how to sell the improved profits resulting from solving a customer's problems through stocks and bonds, certificates of deposit, or life insurance rather than from vending the products themselves.

## Planning Individual Account Penetration

Your decision to concentrate on top-tier penetration requires one more area of sales management expertise. This is a planning function. You must penetrate every key account to its maximum contribution. You must penetrate as quickly as possible because time is money, both for you and for your customer. You must penetrate at high levels to ensure top-tier partnering. You must penetrate on a sequential basis so you will always be at work improving each key account's profit and avoid downtime in applying your talent resources.

There is more. You must penetrate in such a way that you can upgrade your penetrations over time and migrate from them into new opportunities. You must penetrate the most significant customer problems on a priority timetable. In this way, the customer's most compelling needs can benefit first. Furthermore, you will be able to close off invasion routes for your competitors, who will be attracted to any gaps you leave unfilled.

You must accomplish these tasks with every key customer account because it is a miniature market of its own—a microcosm of an industry to which you are committed because you can help it improve its profits and it can help you improve your own.

Each account penetration plan that your representatives prepare is a business plan, a blueprint of how the profit contribution of a customer will be maximized. It is objectives-oriented. The cumulative profit improvement of its strategies adds up to the "product line" you will deliver to the account each year. It tells you how important you are to the customer.

In turn, the improved profit that will accrue to you is your customer's contribution. It tells you how important the customer is to you—how "key" its key account status really is. If your contribution to the customer turns out to be insignificant, you will lose your position as a key source of supply. If the customer's contribution to you is minimal and cannot be improved, you should similarly demote the customer from a key account to a vendor relationship.

## Partnering in Profit

There is only one platform from which you can operate when your objective is to manage your key account penetration for improved profit on sales: Recognize the primacy of improved profit within your key account businesses and make it your No. 1 objective. Of all the dependencies on which key account penetration rests, first and foremost is the creation of a partnership in improved profit making with each customer.

Partnering in mutual profit improvement is the basis for win-win relationships. It requires a dedication to do your up-front homework, to get the facts and quantify their implications in dollar terms. It requires a dedication to install solutions rather than merely sell them. It requires a dedication to put them in place, monitor their contribution, and teach customers how to maintain the contribution at the profit-improving rate you have proposed.

The dedications imposed by a commitment to partner in profit with your key accounts bookend the selling process. At the front end is the requirement to study someone else's business. At the back end are the monitoring, measuring, and teaching requirements that must be carried on with someone else's people. This description may make partnering sound linear, like vendor selling. It is not. Partnering is an endless cycle where homework leads to a proposal, which leads to a sale, which leads to the afterwork following a sale, which leads to upgrading the sale and developing new information about the customer's business, which serves as homework for the next proposal—and so on, endlessly.

Partnering takes place at every stage of the process, because every stage involves the customer's people. The two most productive stages are the discovery of problems that can be solved together and the achievement of their solutions. This reveals the secret of key account partnerships. They are based on two kinds of rewards. One is learning: finding out how to solve a problem that is inhibiting a customer's profits. The other is achievement: proving that a solution works by delivering tangible results to the customer in the form of bankable dollars.

# 2

# Selecting Key Accounts

## *How to Choose Major Customers*

Choosing key customers is a two-step process. The first step is to pick out your natural partners—the customers you are growing right now, who are growing in whole or in part because of you. You can find them by seeking out the heaviest contributors to your profits; if they are growing you, it is because you are growing them.

You should also identify other businesses that are growable by you but that you are not currently growing. This means that they have profitable sales opportunities you can help them exploit or business problems you can help them solve.

How can you know these things? How can you add even more growth to companies you are already growing and how can you pinpoint the most profitable prospective customers to begin to grow?

## Choosing Current Customers With Whom to Partner

There are four questions to answer about your current customers in order to determine which of them you should partner with:

17

1. *Who are we growing right now?* Some of your growth partners will be customers you are already growing, yet you may not be aware of your contribution to their growth. You may think you are merely selling to them in volume at a premium profit. They exist as your prime customers, your key accounts, or heavy users. But they are actually "partners without portfolio." To determine if any one of them should be selected as your partner, you have to answer three more questions.

2. *How much are they growing us?* You may be unable to know the full extent to which you are bringing growth to a current customer. But you can calculate the sum total of profits by which you are growing as a result of doing business with it. There are four standards by which you should measure current customers: their absolute value, their comparative value ranked against your customer list as a whole, their rate of growth, and the trend of their growth rate over the past three years.

3. *How much more can we grow them?* Growth takes place in the future. Consequently, you must add a fifth standard to your calculations: what is the most likely projected rate of improved profits you can plan for in your growth of their business over the next three years? If the projected rate of growth is slowing steadily, becoming static, or declining, you may not have a true growth partner. Instead, you may have a mature customer to whom you should continue to vend product performance values at competitive prices: a customer whom you should sell to and profit from, but with whom you will not grow.

4. *How much more can they grow us?* Because growth partnerships must be reciprocal, you must evaluate the most likely projected rate of profit growth over the next three years to see if it is increasing, becoming static, or declining. If the projected incremental rates of

growth are steadily increasing for both your customer and you, there is a basis for growth partnering.

## Choosing Prospective Partners

There are four questions to answer about prospective partners to determine with which of them you should partner:

1. *Who else can we grow?* Growable businesses that you are not currently growing are your source of market expansion. They may also be a source of diversification. To qualify as a growable customer, a business must meet two criteria: its business problems must be susceptible to significant cost reduction by the application of your expertise and your expertise must be able to increase significantly its profitable sales opportunities.

2. *How much will they grow us?* A business that is growable by you must also be able to grow you in return. Your profit volume and its projected three-year rate of growth must meet or exceed your minimum threshold requirements if you are to avoid opportunity loss.

3. *How can we grow them?* For each growable customer company that you determine to be potentially partnerable, you must plan a growth strategy. The strategy will set forth the precise means by which you will add new profits to its business. You will need to specify how much profit will accrue from reducing costs in its business, how soon the profits will begin, and how long they will continue. You must also be able to specify the total profits from the new sales opportunities you will make available and the markets they can be expected to come from.

4. *What capabilities must we invest in?* Growable

customers that you are not currently growing may demand an extension of your existing capabilities. You may need to fortify your present strengths. You may also need to diversify by adding new strengths in such areas as research, product development, distribution, and human resources. By identifying your "growables" and matching their needs against your capabilities, you answer the questions of whether or not you should diversify, what skills and systems you will need, and how much you will be required to invest in your growth.

Figure 2-1 shows a Partnership Qualification Analyzer. For you and for each prospective partner, the Analyzer allows you to forecast the most likely profit contributions that you can make to a customer and, in turn, the most likely profit contributions he can make to you over a three-year time frame. If these profit flows meet or exceed your own hurdle rate for growth, and if the growth you anticipate for your partner is significant to it, you have the financial basis for partnering.

The profit contribution that you can make to your customer will be the *cause* of the partnership. The profit contribution he makes to you will be its *result*.

## Who Your Partners Are

No matter what business you are in, you have natural growth partners. They are other businesses whose growth is dependent in some significant way on your business. Identifying your growth partners is, overwhelmingly, the most important act of managing your business.

If you know who your natural growth partners are and what they need from you in order to grow, you can

**Figure 2-1. Partnership qualification analyzer.**

Anticipated Profit Contribution to Us by Account

|  | Most Likely Case ($000) | +/− Difference One Year Ago (%) | Worst Case ($000) |
|---|---|---|---|
| 1. *This year* (19__ / 19__) | | | |
| Profit | _____ | ___ | _____ |
| Sales revenues | _____ | ___ | _____ |
| Revenue-to-investment | ___ : ___ | ___ | ___ : ___ |
| 2. *Next year* (19__ / 19__) | | | |
| Profit | _____ | ___ | _____ |
| Sales revenues | _____ | ___ | _____ |
| Revenue-to-investment | ___ : ___ | ___ | ___ : ___ |
| 3. *Third year* (19__ / 19__) | | | |
| Profit | _____ | ___ | _____ |
| Sales revenues | _____ | ___ | _____ |
| Revenue-to-investment | ___ : ___ | ___ | ___ : ___ |

dedicate your businesses to them from the outset. Your business will be a natural response to them. The organizational structure of your profit centers will represent a one-to-one relationship with the customer lines of business that you will grow. Your capabilities will be responses to their needs. Your databases will contain knowledge of their growth problems and opportunities. Your business will be the reciprocal of the business of your partners. For them, as for you, your dealings will be the ultimate in cost-effectiveness.

No business should start up without confirming the

identity of its growth partners. That must be its starting point. The existence of growth partners is the only justification for assuming that a business can be grown. Managers who allege that they have a growth business opportunity should be required to prove it, and the only acceptable proof is the existence of other businesses that can be grown.

If you manage a business that is a going concern, you have two types of natural growth partners. One type is businesses that are currently growing because of you, and the other is businesses that are growable by you but that you are not currently growing. If you are planning a start-up business, all your growth partners will be in the second category.

An up-and-running business tells you who its growth partners are. You will already have discovered them— or, more likely, they will have discovered you, since you may have been selling them your products or processes while they were learning how to apply them to improve their profits. As a result, they are growing because of you. You can find them by segmenting the 20 percent or less of your customers that give you up to 80 percent or more of your profits. You profit from them because they know how to profit from you.

Customers that are already your greatest growth sources are also your greatest potential growth sources. Where there is currently much growth going on, there is prospectively more.

Growth potential is the key partnering criterion. The growth potential of a customer partner determines your own. Only by growing can your partner ensure the fast turnover of your sales to it, along with their continuance. This requires it to have high turnover in the sales it makes to its own customers. If they become stable, its turnover will stagnate. So will yours. For this reason, stable customers—especially those with large shares of market that cannot be grown—are to be avoided like the plague. They may make good customers, but bad partners.

If you have a choice among growable customers, what fine-tuning criteria can you apply to discriminate among them? You should look for three attributes:

1. *Nascent opportunity*. You must seek the maximum opportunity to grow and be grown. Opportunity is the child of change. A growable customer who is undergoing reorganization or restructuring to provide for further expansion is an enhanced partnership prospect. Change at the top is an added enhancement. Whenever major change is taking place, you have the chance to create new roles for yourself, meet new or newly perceived needs in new ways, and form relationships with new managers who can benefit from your expertise.

2. *Positive attitude*. You must prefer to partner with customers who prefer to partner. Their receptivity to your overtures will be greater, and so will their awareness and concern for their costs and revenues. You should expect them to be willing to share data with you and to contribute to your joint database. You should also expect them to create a growth team like yours to ensure that you have access to their decision makers.

3. *High repute*. You must understand that the most sophisticated customers make the best partners. They will have the highest standards of performance. That will push you. They will have the most intelligent leaders in their industry. That will pull you. Your contribution to them will most likely be maximized: they will take what you give them and run with it. Your odds of success will increase, as will your ability to draw on references that will attract other sophisticated customers to you.

Income, impact, and influence are your criteria: a customer with whom mutual growth can be substantial, on whom you can make a major impact that will influence other growth customers to partner with you. Instability in a business, especially restructuring, may make a customer even more attractive.

## Why Your Partners Will Grow You

Partnering requires two choices. One choice is the selection of the customers you will grow. The second choice is made by your customers: Why should they partner with you? Three conditions will motivate them:

1. *You must be an important source of growth profits*. The contribution of new assets that you can make to a customer must be significant. Only then will your partnership be important enough to both of you to merit top-level attention on both sides.

To be an important source of growth means that you must account for worthwhile incremental profits on a customer's bottom line. You must also be able to deliver them in a timely fashion, recognizing the time value of money. In this, you must be dependable. The customer company must be able to count on you to improve its profits when you say you will and by the amounts you promise. Your importance to the customer will be in direct proportion to your reliability.

2. *You must be one of the best investments in profit growth*. A growth partner doing business with you must perceive the price you charge to be an investment rather than a cost. The distinction is vital because only an investment yields a return. He must understand that what he is investing in is not your products or services

or systems, not even your solutions. He will be investing in new profits. The return he receives from the investment must be among the highest yields he can make.

Growth businesses need growers. They need as much growth as they can get as fast as they can get it. They fear the slowing of growth that will come from competitors or the obsolescence of their technological base by new developments. Every day of growth is worth its weight in gold. If your customers' growth rates stabilize, they may never regain fast growth. You, in turn, may never regain them as partners in your own growth.

Just how high does the return on investing have to be? You must compare yourselves with the options. Normally customers will invest in their own businesses in order to make profits. As their partner, you must offer them a better choice. You must make it more profitable to invest in your business. Either the investment they are required to make will be smaller for a similar or greater return, or the return they receive from you will be larger even though the investment may be correspondingly bigger.

3. *You must both have the same competitors.* When you sell products or services, positioning yourselves as one of a customer's alternate vendors, you are only concerned with defeating your own competitors—rival vendors. To be a partner means that you must concentrate on defeating your customer's competitors. Unless you have the same objective you cannot be partners.

Customers' competitors are the constraints on their growth. They have two of them. One is their current costs, against which they compete every day and which they must reduce if they are to improve their profits. You must help them with your expertise. Their second source of competition is the area of sales opportunities. They compete for them every day too, trying to win

customers against their competition. If they are to improve their profits, they must increase their profitable
penetration. Again you must help them with your expertise.

As your partners, your customers will grow you if
you can make three transformations in your relationships
with them.

1. You must first transform yourselves from a supplier of products and services to a supplier of
   profits. You must change yourselves from a manufacturing or service business into a financial
   service company whose product is profits.
2. You must transform yourselves from representing
   an added cost to an added value. You must
   change your basis of doing business from selling
   performance values at a price to returning dollar
   values on an investment.
3. You must transform your outlook from competing
   against other companies in your own business to
   competing against the cost and sales opportunity
   constraints of your partners. You must change
   your objectives to match those of your partners,
   so that you can defeat the same competitors.
   Once you do that, your partners will grow you
   for the same reasons, and in the same ways, that
   they grow themselves.

To help you transform yourselves in these three
ways, you will need a new dictionary—a "partnership
dictionary" that will define the differences between the
language of growth and the languages of manufacturing,
sales and marketing, and competitive vending. As growth
partners, you are expert in growing *markets. Products*

are the new profits you deliver. *Price* is the investment customers make with you to receive the new profits you deliver. The *profit performance* of your products is your partners' return on investment. *Competition* is both your partners' current costs that you must help reduce and current sales that you must help increase.

## What You Must Know to Grow a Partner

"Tell me your asset base and I can tell if you are a grower."

If your asset base is the sum total of your capabilities to manufacture and market—the sum total of your sunk costs—you are probably a vendor. You are growing neither your own business nor the businesses of your customers. If, however, your asset base includes a database of cost and market knowledge about growth customers, you can be a grower. You can grow your own business because you can grow the businesses of your customers.

If you work from a vendor's asset base, you work solely from a source of costs. If you work from a customer database, you work from a source of profits. Within the database are the customer costs you can reduce and the customer sales opportunities you can increase. These are your true growth assets. Without them you can grow neither your customers nor yourself.

The vendors' asset bases drive them. In order to be profitable in spite of typically low, highly competitive vendor margins, their asset bases must achieve low unit costs. To do this, vendors must produce and sell in volume. Whenever supply exceeds demand, margins become depressed. As competitors achieve parity in features, functions, and benefits, price becomes the exclusive means of product differentiation. Margins shrink further as manufacturing costs rise to create a product performance differentiation, and sales costs rise to communicate it. Product presses on vendors. The choice is always between diminished profits from price erosion or from inventory cost. Either way, they cannot grow.

Growers' asset bases drive them too. Because asset-base data are customer data, growers are driven by their customers. Customer costs drive growers to find solutions, to propose them, and to apply them. The amount by which growers can reduce a customer's costs becomes the basis for their price. Customer sales opportunities also drive growers. Potential customer revenues drive growers to find ways to realize them, to propose them, and to bring them in. The sales that growers will develop become the basis for their price.

To be driven by sunk costs is to attempt to escape them. To be driven by customer profits is to attempt to reach out and achieve them. The first strategy is defensive. It will accept stability as the better alternative to decline. The second strategy is aggressive. It will accept only growth.

DATABASE VS. ASSET BASE

Partnered growth is data-driven. Each partner must know the essential growth facts about the other's business. The customer partner must know the supplier partner's capabilities and their most likely impact on his business. The supplier partner must know the customer's business in the two critical dimensions of profit improvement: the customer's business function data, to reduce customer costs; and the customer's market data, to increase customer sales.

The growth facts for a partnership should be a joint

resource. Both partners must contribute to it. The supplier must provide solutions to customer problems by his ability to improve customer profits, and the customer must contribute his supply of cost problems and sales opportunities. Both partners must have equal access to the partnership's growth facts and share the responsibility of ensuring accuracy, currency, and availability.

A jointly held database is second only to jointly achieved profits as the glue that holds a partnership together. The database contains the partnership's agenda: its areas of importance, the problems it can solve and the opportunities it can achieve, and the values that can accrue to the partners.

The partnership database is really two databases. The first is a database on a customer's business function problems—a "cost database." The second is a database on a customer's sales opportunities—a "revenue database" on the customer's customers that compose his own growing and growable partners.

*Business Function Database.* If you are going to improve a customer's profit by reducing costs, you must work from a base of knowledge about them. To be "process smart" about the operations of business, you must know four types of growth facts:

1. *You must know what your competition is.* This means knowing the current costs that are being thrown off by the customer company's operations. It competes against them daily. You must help your customer be a better competitor by learning even more about them. You can help quantify them more exactly. You can also share your knowledge of your own normative costs so the customer company can calculate its variances and bring them into line.

2. *You must have a strategy for applying your expertise against your customer's current costs.* You must know the most cost-effective approach to each problem, its optimal mix of your products and services, and the most expeditious, least disruptive manner of implementing this approach into the customer's operations.

3. *You must know the* norms *for reducing a function's costs by applying your solution.* This means knowing how much of a dollar difference your system can make to a customer's operation before you install it, how quickly the difference will make itself felt, and the degree of assurance you can give that the customer can count on receiving the difference. You must also know how frequently to monitor and measure the difference so that it can be validated.

4. *You must know what a* fair investment *is for the customer to make in exchange for the difference between its current cost and your norm.* This means knowing the value of the difference to the customer: how significant it will be to the value of his business, the added value of the speedy realization of the released funds, and how much it is worth to the customer to have a high degree of certainty that the new profits will flow to you in the promised amounts over the predicted time frame. On this basis you can set a fair price.

*Customer's Customer Database.* If you are going to improve a customer's profit by helping it increase its sales, you must work from a base of knowledge about its markets. To be "market smart," you must know four types of growth facts:

1. *You must first know what your* competition *is.* This means knowing the current profits being contributed by your customer's customers. Because he com-

petes to increase those profits daily, you must help him be a better competitor by learning even more about his customers. You can help him quantify his profits from them more exactly. You can also share your knowledge of his customers' industries so that he can identify his own best growth partners and assign a priority order to partnering with them.

2. *You must have a strategy for applying your* expertise *to increase the customer's current profitable sales from its existing customer base and how to extend that base to new customers.* You must know the most cost-effective approach for each customer market, its optimal mix of your products and services, and the most cost-effective, least vulnerable manner of capturing the market.

3. *You must know the* norms *for increasing a product's sales by applying your kind of solution.* This means knowing how much of a dollar difference your system can make to a customer's product performance before you install it, how long before the difference will make itself felt, and the degree of assurance you can give the customer that it can count on the difference. You must also know how frequently to monitor and measure the difference so that it can be validated.

4. *You must know what a* fair investment *is for the customer company to make in exchange for the difference between its current profits on sales and your norm.* This means knowing the value of the difference to the customer, how significant it will be to the value of the customer's business, the added value of the speedy realization of the incremental funds, and how much the customer values a high degree of certainty that the new profits will flow in the promised amounts over the predicted time frame. On this basis you can set a fair price.

## How to Plan for Your Partnerships

Once you define your business as a growth agent of your partners' businesses, you will have accepted the idea that growth is a joint enterprise. Your growth will be inextricably linked to your partner's growth. Since your growth cannot take place alone, it is foolish to plan it alone.

Partnered growth requires partnered plans for growth. Planning in private, planning from only your own resources, and planning against competitive suppliers instead of planning for your customers are all archaic strategies of growth by conquest, as opposed to growth by collaboration.

Key account penetration plans are the working tools of business that commit their major earnings to each other. They are distinguished from the traditional planning process in two ways: their objectives are mutual and so are the strategies to achieve them.

JOINT OBJECTIVES

When two businesses sit down together to create their plan, neither of them plans its own profit growth. Instead, each plans the incremental earnings it will deliver to the other.

The supplier partner plans the profits he will free up from business function costs in his customer's operations. He also plans the incremental profits from the new sales he will help his customer achieve. The customer partner, in turn, plans the value of the investment he will make in his supplier.

The commitment to accelerate each other's growth forms an implicit contract between the two partners.

Each contracts to be responsible for a specified number of profit dollars that will flow to the other's bottom line. No longer are they simply buyer and seller. Both are now in the business of enriching the other, knowing that they will not be enriched themselves unless they do.

## JOINT STRATEGIES

Shared objectives are the "what" of penetration plans. They are also the "why"—the reason for the partnership. The strategies by which these objectives will be achieved constitute the plan's "how," the means by which mutual profit improvement will take place.

Penetration plans pinpoint the functions in a customer's business where costs can be reduced and where the supplier's expertise, products, and services will be installed to reduce them. A plan should also identify the markets whose profit contribution to the customer will be enlarged as a result of the supplier partner's impact on sales.

Each strategy carries with it a cost. For the supplier, the cost is the total incremental expense of all the components of the strategy: products, services, people, and overhead. This is the supplier's investment in the customer partner. The customer's cost is the combination of the price it pays the supplier plus the internal expenses related to it. This is the customer's investment in the supplier partner.

As with all strategies, joint strategies must be cost-effective. In keeping with the concept of partnership, shared strategies should be good investments. For each partner the investment must be a good deal. That usually means a combination of two of the following three characteristics:

1. *The investment's return must be significant for both partners.* Otherwise one or both of them will suffer an opportunity cost compared to what they might have received in partnership with someone else.

2. *The return must accrue quickly to both partners so that they can turn it over quickly and invest in making even more profits.* A delay in the return will represent additional opportunity cost. To replace the delayed inflow of cash, direct costs of borrowing may be incurred as well.

3. *The certainty of the investment's return must be high.* This must be more than faith. It is the need of each partner for reliability in managing its assets. Both must know when money will be coming in and how much it will be. Money expectations that are not fulfilled may be more disruptive than the assured absence of any incremental cash inflow at all, because money in business is invested—if not in the form of dollars, then certainly in the form of plans—as soon as it is expected.

## How You Can Start Up a Partnership

To start up a key account partnership, you must make the first move. But how? Saying to a customer, "We want to partner with you," is nothing. Saying, "We want to improve your profit—here is how much, here is how, and here is where and when," is to speak to a customer in a way that has meaning.

A system for getting started—a starter kit for growth partnering—consists of eight steps, summarized in Figure 2-2 and outlined below.

*Step 1:* Choose one growth partner. The preferred choice is a customer you are already growing. If your

**Figure 2-2. Partnership start-up steps.**

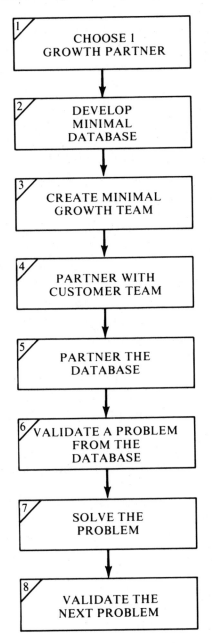

business is a start-up, you will have to choose a customer you believe to be growable.

*Step 2:* Develop a minimal database on the customer's business. Quantify one cost problem in one of its business functions. Alternatively, quantify one sales opportunity in one of its markets for one of its lines of business. Choose a problem or opportunity that can be converted to mutual profit quickly and surely.

*Step 3:* Create a minimal growth team. Choose an entrepreneurial driver to head the team. Staff it with the fewest functional experts required.

*Step 4:* Partner the growth team with a customer growth team as its counterpart. If a cost problem has been identified, partner with the customer business function manager who has responsibility for the problem. If a revenue opportunity has been chosen, partner with the customer profit center manager who has the opportunity.

*Step 5:* Partner the database with the customer's growth team. Validate the quantification of the problem or opportunity.

*Step 6:* Solve the problem and seize the opportunity. Achieve "EVR"—early visible results. Deliver the first growth installment to the customer.

*Step 7:* Suggest the next problem or opportunity. Have it already "in the oven."

*Step 8:* As the second growth installment gets under way, start working with the customer's team on a joint account penetration plan.

An opportunity window for starting up a Key Account Partnership opens when the following conditions are met:

1. The dollar values of the profits from improving a customer's operation exceed the dollar value of the operation's problem.

2. The dollar values of the profits from improving a customer's operation exceed the dollar values of the costs of the improvement.
3. The dollar values of the profits from improving a customer's operation exceed the dollar values of the profits from competitive improvements.

The first condition ensures that a customer problem is worth solving; that is, it is more beneficial to solve it than to ignore it. The second condtion ensures that a problem is profitable to solve. The third condition ensures that a proposed solution will be the preferred solution. All three conditions must be met before partnered growth can get under way.

Getting started in partnering means being an imperfect growth partner. It means partnering in a cost-ineffective manner, accepting errors as the unavoidable price of initiating joint growth with a customer. Errors can be tolerated because, unlike vendor relationships between seller and purchaser, the novice partner has help. The help comes from his customer, who wants him to succeed; he wants him to improve his profit and accelerate his growth. The customer, too, will be an imperfect partner. Only together can they be more profitably grown.

## Tests of Partnering Significance

Partnering is profitable and affordable only with customers that represent present and future growth. These are the customers to whom you are contributing major profits right now. They are also the customers to whom you can contribute major profits in the near future. Each customer from either of these two groups must meet three partnering criteria:

1. *Significance of profit contribution:* A partnership must provide or promise a minimal annual profit. The minimum profit equals or exceeds the partners' hurdle rates for return on investments in their own businesses. Minimum annual profit will depend on the answers to the partner selection test, the prime test of significance you must pass if you are to partner successfully:
   a. Does the customer have major business function costs that you can significantly reduce?
   b. Does the customer have revenue opportunities with major markets that you can significantly increase?
2. *Continuity of profit contribution:* A partnership must provide or promise the accumulation of minimum profits over at least a three-year time frame.
3. *Growth of profit contribution:* A partnership must provide or promise an increasing annual rate of minimum profit increase over its life cycle so that it remains a prime investment option for both partners.

These three criteria will help determine if a prospective partner will meet your partner selection test. In this way, key account partnering forces you to evaluate your customer portfolio according to profit criteria, not according to volume or your share of a customer's business as one vendor among several.

Key account partnering also invites four additional tests of your products, technology, data, and management:

1. *The product test:*
   a. Can your product reduce a significant customer cost?
   b. Can your product increase significant customer sales?
2. *The R&D test:*
   a. Can your technology commercialize products that reduce significant customer costs?
   b. Can your technology commercialize products that increase significant customer sales?
3. *The database test:*
   a. Do you know the dollar values of the costs you can reduce in the customer business functions you affect—and do you know the value to the customer of your solutions?
   b. Do you know the dollar values of the sales opportunities you can increase in the customer markets you affect—and do you know the value to the customer of your solutions?
4. *The management test:*
   a. Do you have the sales teams who can apply your products, support systems, and database to reduce significant customer costs?
   b. Do you have the sales teams who can apply your products, support systems, and data base to increase significant customer sales?

## Platforming the Partnership

Every key account partnership stands on a platform. The partnership platform has two planks. One is composed of the objectives the partners plan to achieve. The other is the strategies they agree on to achieve their objectives. The objectives speak for the *how much* of their growth—where growth will take them. The strategies speak for the *how*—the operations of the customer's business that will be grown and the systems that will be applied to generate growth and to measure it.

It is inherent in the partnership commitment that both partners will accelerate each other's growth. Otherwise, there is no point in partnering. But it is not enough to rest the case for partnership on mutual profit improvement. Each partnership should strive to maximize the partners' growth, not just to add to it. Furthermore, their relationship should maximize their growth better than partnering with someone else would do.

Through this type of platform a partnership becomes institutionalized. It takes on the identity of a business alliance, not a fly-by-night contrivance of dubious dedication or duration. Theoretically, a key account partnership should endure as long as both partners realize the purposes they have expressed in the platform. Every day they maximize their growth, the partnership is working.

## OBJECTIVE

Partnerships are profit maximizers. That is how the partners grow each other and, in turn, themselves. The volume of profits that they generate is therefore paramount. A partnership that is a heavy profitmaker is preferable to a light earner. If it is a consistently heavy profitmaker, it will be even more preferred.

Earning profits in volume is maximizing growth. Earning profits quickly and recurrently is minimizing the time within which growth can take place. The time value of money as well as its dollar value must be recognized in the objectives of partners who agree to increase each other's wealth.

A third factor also deserves consideration: the certainty of growth. It will be evidenced in the strategies the partners decide to focus on, matching the customer partner's profit problems and opportunities with the supplier partner's capacity to solve some of the problems and capitalize on some of the opportunities.

Growth partners always have the same needs. They each want to maximize new profits and they want them on a continuing basis with plannable certainty. This is the motivation that brings them together in partnership. But method is different from motivation. The method by which both partners prosper is for both of them to grow the customer partner—the sole source of partnered growth.

The object of key account partnerships must be maximizing growth of the customer. There is no other way a partnership can succeed. This is not a sales strategy on the part of the supplier, but basic operating strategy, which permits no deviation. To lapse from it is to relapse into vending. All objectives for the partnership must therefore begin with growing the customer. The supplier's growth is derived growth, resulting from customer growth and totally dependent on it.

Maximized customer growth is the conceptual basis for partnered growth objectives. Growth objectives are not just hopes and promises. If growth is to be real, it must be quantified as incremental profit dollars, which represent the value added by the partnership to the customer. They allow the customer to self-generate growth funds, realizing them from the costs that the partnership has reduced and from the sales revenues the partnership has increased.

The overall growth objective for the customer partner must be broken down into its two component parts. Part one is profit growth from solving cost problems in the customer's operations. Which business functions will compose the partnership's arena? Which costs? By how much will they be reduced? Part two is profit growth from capitalizing on sales opportunities for the customer. Which markets will compose the partnership's arena? Which product lines sold to them? By how much will their revenues and earnings be increased?

Only after the customer's objectives have been planned can the supplier partner plan its own growth objectives.

The customer's objectives are really the return on the investment it makes in partnering. The supplier's growth will come from that investment. The customer's return must maximize his use of money: the return must be a good deal. Similarly, the investment that the customer makes in the supplier constitutes the supplier's return. It must also maximize the supplier's use of money so that it represents a good deal for the supplier, too.

Key account partnerships succeed when they are a good deal for both partners. Each wins. If only one can win, there is no basis for partnership.

## STRATEGY

Objectives quantify the extent to which profit will be improved. Strategies specify how and where: whether a cost will be reduced or revenues improved in the customer business functions to which the supplier will apply his capabilities.

The master strategy for growing a customer partner is to improve its profits. This is accomplished by a portfolio of proposals that will reduce its costs or increase its revenues. The substrategies of growth partnering are *cost reduction* and *revenue gain*. If cost is expressed as investment and revenues are translated into profits, these two substrategies will be the components of return on investment. Either one or both will affect profits.

Cost reduction strategies require agreement on the selection of customer business functions where economies can be introduced, freeing the released funds for other uses. Proposing cost reduction presupposes knowledge of how a customer's costs are generated: labor costs, work flow processing costs, material costs, manufacturing costs, sales and distribution costs, communications costs—whatever costs a supplier can affect. If cost reduction is going to be your contribution to a partnership, you must be expert in the customer's operations.

Revenue-improvement strategies require agreement on the selection of customer markets in which sales can be increased to bring in new funds. Proposing revenue gain presupposes knowledge of the customer's markets in which sales opportunities exist for increased turnover of existing products or increased penetration of new products. If revenue gain is going to be your contribution to a partnership, you must be expert in customer sales development.

When customer candidates for partnership ask a prospective supplier how he proposes to grow their businesses, they are asking him to position himself as a potential growth partner. Does he propose to grow them in the role of a cost reducer? If so, what does he know of their current costs and by how much can he reduce them? Or does he propose to grow them in the role of a sales developer? If so, what does he know of their current sales and by how much can he improve them?

The supplier's answers to these questions will be his profit-improvement proposals. Each proposal will make three statements: Here is something I know about your business, either a function that is overcosted or a market that is undersold. This is how much growth I can bring to it. Here is how I can do it.

The only true growth is profit growth. Volume growth may yield profit growth, but in itself it represents only added cost.

Market share growth is volume growth. The dollar value of each successive share of market reaches an optimal point and then undergoes diminishing returns as the costs to push beyond that point rise in disproportion to their yield. Growth through a customer's sales function can be complicated because of these often inverse relationships between the incremental costs of volume and the incremental profits that can be made from new revenues.

In contrast, reducing a customer's costs to improve his profit is relatively straightforward. Dollar for dollar, reduced costs can drop undiminished to the bottom line.

## How You Can Inaugurate a Growth Network

Key account partnering gives you the opportunity to initiate a prosperous economic microcosm composed of the customers and customer's customers you partner with. No matter what the state of the economy may actually be, you can be the inaugurators of a profitable enclave within it in which growth is shared, one business with another.

A growth network begins when you start to grow a customer partner. To the extent that you grow him he will cause you to grow. He will increase his investment with you. You will prosper. The two of you will have

**Figure 2-3.  A growth network.**

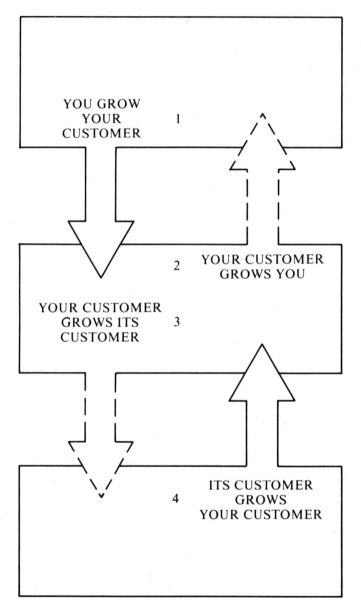

formed a growth cell. Once that occurs you will be ready to reproduce growth by adding other cells to your net.

The primary way you grow your customer partner will be through improving his profits from sales. No matter how much you reduce his costs, his growth will always be largely dependent on sales. Inevitably you will be helping grow his own customers. They, in turn, will force growth back upon him. Each of your customer partners will have two growth sources: You will be one and his partnered customers will be the other. In this way additional growth cells will be formed.

A customer-centered growth network is illustrated in Figure 2-3. It shows the four steps it takes to create two growth cells. In steps one and two, you grow a customer and the customer grows you. In steps three and four, the customer grows one of his customers and his customer grows him. As additonal growth cells are added to the network, more growth is created through progressive partnering.

# 3

# Selling at High Margins

## *How to Reach the Customer's Top Tier*

High-margin selling to key account decision makers is a business of its own. It requires a sales strategy composed of skills that are mostly at a 180-degree variance from vendor skills. It requires sales representatives who are recruited according to consultant characteristics and who are supported, compensated, and managed in a different way from vendors. They do not "yes . . . but" their way to overcome customer objections, they do not trial close, and they do not sell price performance, because they do not sell products.

In order to penetrate their customers at high management levels where high margins are obtainable, key account sales representatives must be trained in the Consultative Selling skills, that is, the agenda for what takes place when the key account representative stands before the customer tier at the top. This is no-man's land for the vendor sales representative. To sell at this level, only "the product of your product" can be sold—that is, only the improved profit it can deliver. How well a key account representative has learned this is revealed by

47

how long it takes him to complete the five-step Consultative Selling cycle.

There are two prime duties of your key account representatives: to become proficient in Consultative Selling skills and to learn how to turn over the Consultative Selling cycle in the most rapid manner.

The sales management level is the most vital support source for key account representatives. It is true that they can sell without the three contributions that sales management should make to them. But you will pay the price. The best of your current force will leave and go elsewhere to a more conducive, more fully committed environment. The best of your candidates will prefer to sign on elsewhere. They have learned what to ask for up front. The rest will probably stay. That is where you will pay the price.

What support do you need to provide? You must stake out a corporate position as the educator of your key customer industries on how they can improve profits, cost reduction, and productivity in the areas of their businesses that you affect. You must reach out and fertilize your total marketing strategy with the Consultative Selling platform of key account penetration. Further, you must indoctrinate the nonselling functions in your company as well.

This triple-barreled approach will maximize the value of the training you provide in Consultative Selling skills. It will apply your company's resources against the customers who are its main sources of earnings. It will help safeguard your key account businesses from competition. And last but not least, it will give you the single best selling edge in your industry: It will define your business in relation to the central needs of your key customers, the needs they have to increase their profits.

## Standing Before the Tier at the Top

Top-tier customer management rarely deals with vendors and then only under duress. They speak different languages. Vendors speak price and performance benefits. Management speaks value and profit contribution. Vendors speak costs. Management speaks return on investment. Vendors speak of their competitors. Management is concerned about its own. Vendors wonder when management will ever buy. Management wonders when vendor presentations will ever end.

Vendors who stand before their customer tier at the top will not do so for long or soon again. For consultative sellers to make a stand, and make it again and again, they must be prepared to speak the language of management, address its concerns instead of their own, and put to work their knowledge of the customer's business so that a demonstrable improvement—not just a shipment of goods—takes place.

Figure 3-1 shows the composition of the top management tier and the decision-making criteria it reacts to at its top and upper-middle levels. In contrast, the criteria of the purchasing tier are markedly different.

Key account sales representatives who want to penetrate the top customer tier must position themselves to discuss, document, and deliver their answers to the question "How much profit will you add?" For them, that is their sales mission in a nutshell. It is what being a key account sales representative is all about. A mix of three skills is required for them to take the consultative position. One is the skill of knowing the customer's business well enough to know how a profit is made and how it can be improved. A second skill is demonstrating an improvement. The third skill is creating the close, continuing partnerships on the top tier that foster on-

**Figure 3-1. Top-tier decision-maker criteria.**

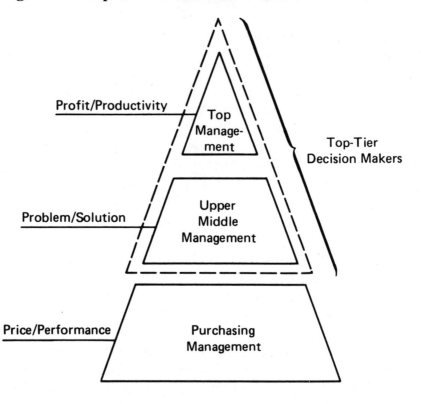

going knowledge of the customer's business and guarantee the availability of top-tier managers to receive the sales representatives' proposals.

The key account representatives who stand before customer management as consultants assume a hybrid stance. They are not vending. They cannot be positioned as traditional sellers. Nor are they managing their customer's business. They cannot be positioned as peers. Above the one, they are below the other. Their closest analog is among the customer's own middle-management staff, not with anyone else from the outside. Internal people who report to the top tier, who bring financially quantified solutions to it for proposal and disposal, and who must then implement them when they are budgeted provide the key account sales representatives' most approximate role models.

Internal managers most often approach their top tier as the principals in a four-act play. Key account sales representatives should follow this scenario closely, both in sequence and in content.

## ACT 1: "WHY DO YOU WANT TO SEE ME?"

Everyone who approaches top-tier management must offer justification. Management's brainpower is every company's most precious internal resource. It must be profitably engaged every minute. Down time is time lost forever. Management knows what is profitable. "Do *you?*" it asks. Management knows what needs improvement to become more profitable. Do *you?*

Your sales representatives must be prepared to declare what they want to see their customer decision makers about. It must be a problem of significant customer concern or it must be a major opportunity. It must be current, and be the kind of situation that appears solvable within a reasonable amount of time. Issues that meet these criteria are top-tier management's proper business. Any other issues—specifically those within the sales representatives' business—will bring the response that management is too busy with its own business to deal with them. Act 1 can be the final act unless the customer's business is spotlighted on center stage.

## ACT 2: "WHAT DO YOU WANT ME TO DO ABOUT IT?"

Management-level decision makers make decisions. They do not contemplate idly. When you raise an issue with management, you cannot provoke curiosity without offering a cure. Once management knows why you want its attention and agrees on the merit of your response, it must know next what you want it to do. Your sales representatives will, of course, end up doing something about the issues they raised. But management must do something first: It must appropriate assets in the form of dollars and people.

Assets are allocated for solutions, either solutions that prevent problems or those that can relieve problems in whole or in part. Management must be told what solutions are available to it. Some may already have been tried and failed. Should any of them be considered anew? Some attempts at solution may already be in implementation. Can they be reinforced? Should they be superseded before they fail or prove cost-ineffective? Is there a best solution—if so, how can you tell it is best? What can its contribution be expected to amount to?

When customer management evaluates solutions, it is not evaluating products, services, or systems. It may know little about them and care less. Top management assesses only the financial results of a solution, not its components or their performance. Operating managers will be more interested in both. But at the top, the dialogue of Act 2 will be principally in the dollar terms of how much profit you are prepared to offer management and how much, in return, you want as your reward.

ACT 3: "HOW DO I KNOW IT WILL WORK?"

If management likes what you want it to do—in other words, if it likes the amount of added profit you promise—it will want to know how it can realize your proposal. "How do I know the profits you promise will actually accrue?" That is what top management means by "Will it work?" Whether the gears will mesh or the system will integrate will have to be demonstrated to operating management. At the top tier, a proposal works when it produces the profit output claimed for it. If it operates mechanically, chemically, or electronically but the profits are not forthcoming, it does not work.

In Act 3, your key sales representatives must attest to the workability of their solution. They must document the customer's prospective profits, showing their source, their flow, and their cumulative total. Your key sales representatives must also attest to the overall composition of their solution. In general, what major product components will it contain? What services? What does the system as a whole look like? How does it conform to state-of-the-art technology, and what is its track record? The specifics of its features and benefits will be relegated to the probings of operating management "downstairs."

Act 3 can therefore be divided into two sequential scenes. First, operating managers should be partnered on the performance contributions of your proposals. Then, when agreement has been reached with them, the financial contributions should be proposed to top management. This phasing of approval permits top management to obtain the immediate concurrence of its operating decision makers: "Is this what you want? Will it work the way they say it will?" It also prevents incurring resentment at the operating levels from having a decision handed down instead of participating in handing it up.

## ACT 4: "WHEN DO WE GET THE SHOW ON THE ROAD?"

When your key account sales representatives sell consultatively, buying action will most likely come from the customer in Act 4. As soon as your solution is perceived to work financially and operationally, top management will want to implement it. Time is money. Every minute's delay deprives top management of promised profits.

Implementation consists of four elements. The first three concern what will be installed, when it will become operational, and who from each side will be involved. The fourth element is the sum total of the first three. What resources will have to be provided from the customer's business to match the resources contributed by the team of your key account representative and support services? Only when people—their time and talent—and money are allocated does something get done. You must be prepared to specify what both of you will have to put up in order to get the show on the road.

Your key account representatives must be trained to produce their four-act plays at a fast clip, requiring a minimum of props, and moving smoothly from one act to the next. Like all good plays, profit-improvement proposals should be presented orally, with a copy of the libretto for each member of the audience. An hour, allowing time for interruptions, is the maximum length any performance should require. The audience has other plays to go to. As for your own people, they earn their pay only when they implement—not when they propose.

Where are the trapdoors under top management's carpet? They are everywhere. Act 1 can close out your performance if you focus on a problem that customer management does not perceive as significant or if you fail to describe a truly significant problem correctly in management terms. You will be dismissed as not understanding the customer's business.

If the solution you propose in Act 2 pays out too little profit or is too late in coming, it may be rejected. If it is too great in amount, your credibility may be suspect.

Can you really do what you say you can do? If you are deemed not credible, you will not be trusted with management's approval. Even worse, if your solution appears to be unlikely and you provide supportive testimony from another industry, even though closely allied, or another company in your customer's industry, you may be summarily dismissed as not understanding the differences between your customer's business and all others.

In the event that fault is found with your financial documentation of profit contribution in Act 3, especially if the errors are in your favor, your image or your credibility will be downgraded. You may nonetheless survive if the corrected contribution remains significant. If your profit analysis fails utterly, you will be dismissed as not understanding the first thing about the business of consultation in profit improvement.

Act 4 is the proof of the pudding. If you cannot implement, you will be dismissed as not understanding the second thing about the business of how to bring profits down to a customer's bottom line.

## Five-Stepping the Consultative Selling Cycle

A key account sales representative going through the Consultative Selling cycle will take five steps. They are all forms of learning and teaching. The cycle contains two types of elements. Planning the account's penetration and generating the proposal are the least time-consuming elements. But the other three elements are dependent on customer people: their cooperation, their information, and their instigation of acceptance inside the customer's organization structure. When the selling cycle turns over slowly, people problems are probably the reason. This puts a premium on the ability of key account representatives to achieve multiple partnerships with operating, financial, and managerial levels in their accounts.

The five-step selling cycle starts with databasing and proceeds to penetration planning, preliminary partnering, proposing, and implementing. As logic suggests, these steps are generally sequential. Frequently, however, databasing must be returned to, planning must be revised, and initial partnerings must be reinstituted with different influencers or decision makers. In these instances, the cycle is less of a progressive curve than a zigzag.

## STEP 1: DATABASING

Knowledge of the customer's business is the basis for penetration planning, partnering, and proposing. Two things can usually be said about it. Unlike product knowledge, you probably do not have sufficient customer knowledge at the start. And, again unlike product knowledge, you probably cannot acquire the customer knowledge you need, or validate the knowledge you have, without getting into the customer's business. From the very outset, partnering skills are crucial.

The vital components of your key customer database are twofold. The first component is the customer's currently perceived critical problems and opportunities in the business functions you can affect. What are they, where are they, what are the dollar values the customer has put on them, and who are the decision makers who will determine what action, if any, is to be taken about them? The second component is the customer's currect solutions. What are they, what are the dollar values attributed to them, where are they deficient, and who are their advocates?

When you have digested these two areas of information, you will be able to add a third component to your database. What are your own solutions to the customer's problems and unachieved opportunities, and what are the incremental dollar values they can contribute when compared against the customer's current solutions?

## STEP 2: PENETRATION PLANNING

The database predetermines each key account's penetration plan and the partnering and proposing that execute it. That is why key account selling is data-dependent. The plan deals with the data on an as-if basis: *as if* the data are the customer's business as far as your sales opportunity is concerned. It then asks and answers the following questions:

What is your optimal solution for each customer problem and opportunity? What is its dollar value to the customer? To you? What is it composed of—what products and services? Is it a superproduct, as discussed in Appendix I? Who are the decision makers involved? What is the total contribution you can make to this customer? What is the customer's total expected contribution to you? What is your revenue-to-expense ratio to achieve it?

The penetration plan is your operating manual with each account. It should serve two purposes. It will allow you to manage the account's penetration, determining how much of its potential contribution you are reaching, whether or not you are on schedule, and what unexploited opportunities remain for proposing. This is the plan's internal function. It should have an external use as well. It should be positioned by your key account representatives as the mutual plan of their partnerships with customers. Each representative should prepare the plan with customer participation, making sure that its priorities and assumptions are those of the account. The representative should be equally certain that customer decision makers understand how much profit improvement he expects to bring them and what their own commitment of resources will have to be if they want it.

## STEP 3. PRELIMINARY PARTNERING

Partnering begins when your key account representatives share their penetration plans with customer decision makers and influencers. From there, it must go on to include appropriate division and department managers; financial administrators; functional managers in sales, engineering, and manufacturing; and operating managers.

With each category of management, mutual objectives must be established and agreements reached on the most acceptable strategic approach to achieve them. Information must be encouraged to flow both ways so that everybody contributes something to your customer database and everybody takes something away, only to return it in more accurate, fact-enriched form.

Partners will emerge in several guises. Information partners will show and tell but do nothing. Action partners will work with your representatives but will not necessarily go to bat for them. Contrariwise, advocate-type partners will speak for your representatives at high customer levels but will play no active role in getting the work done. Somewhere along the line, your sales representatives will have to identify their mentor partners, who will guide them through the customer's political and social systems, steering them to supporters and away from delayers or apparent nay-sayers.

Partnering at many different position levels with many different personalities, professional cultures, and political relationships is a complex task. It is the key account sales representatives' master skill. Unless they can correlate their mission with each potential partner's own objectives and create a participative strategy that takes those objectives into consideration, they will essentially be reduced to vending, no matter what other skills they may possess.

## STEP 4. PROPOSING

Each proposal to improve a key account's profit or productivity or operating performance should be one of the modules in the account's penetration plan. It should bear a priority ranking and, whenever possible, flow out of a previous proposal and into a following one. The knowledge of what to propose, to whom it should be proposed, and when the proposal should be made must come out of customer partnering.

Each proposal should be looked on as serving three purposes. The first purpose is to sell at a high-margin price that is commensurate with the customer's improved profit. Second, a proposal should prepare the way for its follow-on proposals. Third, successful proposals should be recycled into your database so that they can be used over and over again as references for proposals yet to come.

## STEP 5. IMPLEMENTING

Proposals are born in data and mature in profitability or perish in implementation. No matter how optimal your solution may be, it is valueless if its integration into the customer's business does not make the full contribution of profit you have proposed.

Implementation is the acid test of your ability to convert promise into performance. It is your main chance to cement partnerships, earn your way into further learning about the customer's business, and be first in line to propose your next strategy to improve customer profit.

No matter what business you are in, and no matter what specific aspects of integrating your solutions you must depend on, there are three common denominators of implementation to which you must adhere.

As quickly as possible, you must install your solution in the customer's operations. It must start to function. It must begin to produce the profit stream you have proposed. The onset of profit is the crucial element of implementation. Every day of delay—in many situations, every hour and every minute—has a dollar equivalent that subtracts from the promise of your proposal. Conversely, every day of incremental profit is a bonus.

Monitoring your solution, not just its operating performance but also its delivery of improved profit, must go hand in glove with your installation. Your sales representatives and their customer partners will have to agree beforehand on the criteria for monitoring exactly what is expected and the milestones when it is due. A monitoring system and periodic joint progress meetings are necessary to ensure common perceptions of what is being achieved.

Finally, there can be no implementation without training the customer's people how to operate the solution, maintain it, and measure its contribution. Training helps ensure the achievement of your proposal. It spares your customer an added cost, thereby increasing profit.

Similarly, it also spares you the added cost of providing endless service, repairs, and warranteed replacement parts due to customer ineptitude that can seriously injure your own profit on sales.

The beginning point of every Consultative Selling cycle is clear: It is always data based. But when does a cycle end? It is tempting to say that the customer acceptance of your proposal is the natural end point. But getting the customer's improved profits to flow during implementation is really the signal that your original promise is on the way to realization. This earns you the right to propose once again, initiating a new cycle as the next stage of an endless process of profit improvement.

## Preempting the Industry Educator Position

A key account sales organization is a mighty information machine. When it is industry-based, it learns a lot about each customer industry it serves—industry economics, key financial ratios, performance averages and norms, market trends and projections. It is customer-intensive as well, so it learns a great deal about each key account—financial ratios, performance averages and norms compared to industry criteria, trends, projections, and an account's customer markets.

There are two constituencies for this wealth of information, in the form of either raw data or reports to which you have added some value by custom-tailored processing. For industry data, the industries themselves present you with a potential market. So do companies that may be searching out growth opportunities outside their own industries. For customer data, you may have two markets: the customers themselves, for whom their own information will be the basis for proposals to improve their profit; and your customer's own key account representatives.

The raw materials stockpiling, manufacture, and distribution of this information, both for internal and external consumption, offers a correlate to the stockpiling, manufacture, and distribution of your products. It enables you to take a position as the preeminent source of industry information supply.

In order to dominate an industry's perception of you as knowledgeable in its business, there is no substitute for being its preemptive educator. Key account selling is knowledge-based selling. To sell from knowledge, there are two requisites. You must have the data. You must also have the repute for having the data. If you meet the requisites, you provide your sales force with the benefit of selling from an acknowledged industry-smart platform.

The answer to the question "What is the best positioning for a key account sales strategy?" is that you should become recognized as the leading educator in each industry you want to penetrate. There are three approaches to accomplishing this objective.

1. *The institute approach.* Your industry database can become the core of a business unit called an institute: the Institute of Productivity Improvement if you sell office product systems, the Institute of Risk Management if you sell fire-protection systems, the Institute of Critical Care Therapeutics if you sell hospital equipment. The institute can be set up as a quasi-independent but wholly owned subsidiary. It should distribute its information free from overt sales contamination through multiple media such as books, magazines, newsletters, videofilms and discs, seminars and conferences, and traveling road shows. Customers and prospects alike are

its audience. If your business is involved with a public service such as environment or energy, this can be featured. The involvement of your products is legitimate wherever they fit the message.

2. *The corporation-as-educator approach*. With or without an institute, the corporation itself can benefit the key account sales thrust by dedicating its overall position to educating its markets. The corporate theme should emphasize this dedication. So should the architectural layout of corporate headquarters. The main entrance can, for example, show the optimal use of corporate products at a customer location under actual conditions, supplemented by photographs and continuous films. The annual report and executive meetings with investment analysts, advertising of both product and institutional types, and public relations can all be used to propagate the educator position. You and your key account representatives should author articles for customer industry media, speak at its conventions, and demonstrate your educational contributions at its trade shows and exhibits.

3. *The sales force as learners/teachers approach*. Key account sales representatives are teachers of profit improvement to customer decision makers. If they teach well, they will sell well. To teach well, they must be taught well. A key account sales organization must therefore be a year-round educational organization whose curriculum is customer profit improvement based on Consultative Selling skills.

All new key account sales representatives should be taught consultative skills. This is ingrade training. All practicing key account representatives should be periodically retrained in the skills that enable them to be properly positioned, to prepare profit-improvement proposals, and to be good business partners with their customers. This is upgrade training. The same kind of training should be given to regional and district sales managers and all national account managers. Outside the sales force, Consultative Selling skills should be communicated to product development people, financial people, managers of marketing functions, and your own top management—your own top tier—so they will know how to support your key account sales operations.

This three-pronged approach evidences many things to your constituents. To current and prospective key account customers, it underscores your enduring interest in their industry and validates your capability base for providing them with substantive help. To your key account sales force, it proves your long-term commitment to support Consultative Selling strategies with their high-level customers. For potential new hires, it fortifies the belief that you offer a competitively superior career path. And finally, to your own upper levels of management, it helps position their business, allocate proper funds to support your key account plans, and take on some consultative characteristics themselves when they sell to upper-level customers in their stratospheric contacts.

## Fertilizing the Total Marketing Strategy

In most companies, selling is regarded as a subservient marketing function. Others hedge, marrying sales and marketing in a single function. In technical companies, marketing tends to be a support function for sales. What is marketing anyway?

Marketing is the creation of customer perceptions of premium value for a business. Since high-margin prices are the reward for perceived premium value, marketing strategy obviously has the ability to make a serious positive or negative impact on selling to key accounts. Total marketing strategy must be made supportive to key customer penetration.

Marketing itself, as an amalgam of functions, should be a key account process. Unlike the sales function, marketing has no bottom-tier constituency. Perceptions of premium value need to be created only among the market segments—the key industries—where Consultative Selling will take place. No one else needs to be marketed to, since industries that are not key—because they are not among the 20 percent or so that provide up to 80 percent of profitable sales volume—will not be asked to pay premium prices for vended values.

Once marketing is seen as a key account function, urgency for close correlation of its component functions with key account selling will become apparent.

The key account selling database is industry-dedicated and customer-oriented. It can therefore easily become the marketing database as well, since the same industries and the same companies will be marketed to. Marketing, like all corporate functions, must be market-driven. This will unfailingly be the case when it is allied to real, live data about its major markets, separately by one or another of its component functions that may be in organizational favor at any given time.

Marketing's prime standard of performance must be to support key account sales penetration. If it cannot do this, it can do nothing. The marketing plan's goal should be providing optimal support to achieve the combined objectives of all the individual account penetration plans and delivering this support in the most cost-effective manner. The standard of performance for marketing cost-effectiveness is achieved when upward revisions in marketing allocations would not proportionately increase key account profit contribution to you; con-

versely, downward revisions would decrease your key
account profits in a disproportionate ratio.

This perspective of marketing harnesses it to sales,
exactly the opposite of traditional policy in companies
that practice vendor sales to both top and bottom tiers
throughout all the industries they serve. Every other
function in a company, the nonselling functions as well
as marketing, should be equally supportive of key account selling, since they all depend on its revenues for
their sustenance.

As key account penetration becomes increasingly
important to your business growth strategy, two-tier
selling and, along with it, top-tier concentration will
become your fundamental sales strategy. Fallout strategies from it will affect your marketing function. There
will be less and less mass marketing, since mass markets
will continue their present fractionalization into more
and more finite segments. Along with the shortage of
mass markets will be vast reductions in full product lines
that offer something for everybody. Production, marketing, and sales will stringently focus on the big winners in
every line and let the others slide. Marketing will then
no longer have to keep every product and market manager happy by supporting full lines and stroking every
customer industry in the corporate portfolio.

There are five components of total marketing strategy that must be fertilized, that is, correlated with your
key account sales penetration strategy. Marketing will
have to concentrate on key industries; key customer
accounts within each key industry; and the big winner
products, services, and systems sold to them. It will
have to support the key account penetration selling
strategies in each industry, using the same sales style of
customer profit improvement and the same sales content
that offers documentation. In every instance, the crunch

criterion will have to be "Does what we are doing support our key account sales representatives—does it help shorten their Consultative Selling cycle with top-tier customer decision makers and more quickly enable them to make more sizable high-margin sales?"

## ADVERTISING AND SALES PROMOTION

Key account sales strategy requires key account two-tier advertising strategy. All other sales and advertising should vend. Advertisements and sales promotion brochures, catalogues, and product announcements directed to purchasing agents and engineering-acculaturated functional managers such as data processing managers, telecommunications managers, risk managers, equipment standardization committee managers, and the like should be price-performance advertisements. Features and benefits should prevail over claims of profit improvement except in the case of markets where the purchasing-type functions are being educated to demand profit, cost, or productivity benefits along with performance results.

Advertising and collateral sales support materials designed for top-tier decisions makers at key customer accounts will be completely different. They will be profit-themed. Products and systems may not even be shown. You should not proclaim your own ability to improve customer profits, nor should your key account "experts" or their support staffs be starred as the instigators of better bottom lines. Instead, advertising should showcase your key customers. Profit improvement claims should be their claims, testimony their testimony, results their results. They should have high appetite value to make your other key customers and prospects hunger for similar infusions of new profits.

Consultative Selling advertises itself by the case method, which serves many purposes. It documents your profit-improvement capability; promotes your track record; professionalizes your consultative approach, freeing you from the need to blow your own horn; and at the same time, it stimulates your customers to ask their key account representatives the opening question "Can you do the same thing for us?"

PRODUCT NOMENCLATURE

For the vendor market, the name of a product or system is probably inconsequential. So tangential is the usual impression that most vended products are unnamed. They bear only serial numbers or letters, like the 3000 or the Series J. If there are names, they most likely describe what the product is, such as a Spectrum or a Port-O-Cath or a New Dimension, instead of what it does that can help improve customer profit.

In key account selling, product or process names can have an additive effect on penetration if they are correlated with improved customer profit. Big winner products should be named with their eventual contribution in mind as a component in a profit-improvement system. The same reasoning applies to names for product-related services for maintenance, upgrading, resupplying consumables, and leasing. What do their names say about their contribution to the system's mission— what synergy does their nomenclature add to the system as a whole?

If the same product is to be marketed to key customers and vended to all others, no problem is created. It can be named for its key account mission and serialized for the other. It can also be painted in different colors for each segment, packaged differently, and otherwise distinguished.

## TRADE SHOWS AND INDUSTRY EXHIBITS

If advertising can be described as selling by other means, so can your appearances at trade shows and industry exhibits. What applies to advertising should apply to them too. Your show themes should teach key customers about your profit-improvement capabilities. Advertised case histories can be collated for distribution and shown in continuous video formats. If your products lend themselves to participative demonstrations, you can permit prospective customers to prove their profit-improving effect for themselves in a hands-on manner.

Trade shows are widely used to collect alleged leads—generally names and inquiries you follow up in an inverse ratio to their number. This probably works out well, because the 80-20 rule suggests that the bulk of them will result in either no sale or only marginally profitable sales. If you are seeking vending leads, following up every contact may be justifiable. But if you want to position your appearance to reinforce key account sales, you will want to find ways to zero in on key customers as distinct from—and perhaps even to the exclusion of—other customer prospects.

What you say about yourself as a profit improver, what you show and teach about your abilities and their results, along with the consultative manner in which you communicate your mission, will be self-selecting. It can either bring you a new record number of unconvertible names or a few new key customers who are highly convertible at high margins.

## ANNUAL REPORT

The 10-K is a legal document. Its market is the Securities and Exchange Commission and the investment community. The annual report is a marketing document. Among its other intended audiences, you key customers look to it for a restatement of your commitment to them, for additional case materials and news about the strengthening of your capabilities, information about your continuing education program in Consultative Selling, fertilization of your nonselling functions with profit-improvement knowledge and motivation—to learn, in short, how seriously you take your partnership position. Security analysts do the same.

Most annual reports are product catalogues. Some show the factory. Among the worst are reports that attempt to humanize their companies: ''All we are is people,'' they say, and that is what they display. Focusing on products, processes, plants, and people all ingnore the source of the funds that pay for them, the key customers they serve. Every year's annual report should be a report card to your key accounts on how you helped them improve their profits again last year, adding, in the best way possible, to the values of your shareholders and theirs as well. Within that context, your people, products, and plants can take on properly contributory meanings.

## EXECUTIVE SPOKESMEN

Your own top-tier executives can be carriers of your profit-improvement mission statement in their appearances before key industry groups and in one-to-one sessions with their peers in your key customer companies. On the other hand, they can deposition you in one fell swoop. Their conversion is the final link in your chain of marketing strategies to support key account penetration.

Today's board chairmen, presidents, and other top-level managers still tend to come from a corporate culture where big was best; where market share and volume bespoke success; and where breadth, diversity, and mass were the magic words. You must help educate them in the dynamics of key account selling based on a consultative approach to their peer top-tier decision makers. If you succeed, they can be the most powerful converts to your side. They also have the ears of other powerful decision makers in your key customer companies who, as influencers, can shorten the cycle for your key account sales representatives.

These five challenges to fertilize your total marketing strategy represent the hardest sell of all—selling the doctrine of key account penetratin internally. It is a classic example of top-tier selling. As such, it will provide an excellent test of your Consultative Selling skills.

## Indoctrinating the Nonselling Functions

Companies that are the ablest penetrators of their key customers make Consultative Selling a corporate policy, not just a sales strategy. They convert their entire organizations into improvers of customer profit, starting with the sales and marketing functions that lay hands on their key acounts and working inward to the nonselling functions. They make everyone customer-sensitive, customer-responsive, and customer-serving.

A unified front gives key account representatives total corporate support over and above functional sales and marketing support. It gives the customer a concerted set of attitudes and behavior patterns to deal with. The pressure the customer feels to improve profits is consistent. All your people carry the same message. Each time they do business with the customer, they want to leave improved profits behind.

The three nonselling functions most essential for you to bring over to the consultative way are research and development, product or service engineering, and finance.

## RESEARCH AND DEVELOPMENT (R&D)

Key account penetration strategy reaches its zenith when it permeates the laboratory. Instead of building products and process that offer scientific challenge—that are built because they can be built better than anyone else can build them—penetration stategy gets to steer development in the direction of offering maximum profit improvement to your major markets. Customer approval rather than the envy or admiration of competitive scientists becomes the foremost R&D objective.

Research must be taught to make what can be sold consultatively; that is, what can be sold at high margins because of superior ability to improve customer profit. This requires R&D to be a consumer of market fact and a heavy user of the key account knowledge banks of customer problems and opportunities. Customer knowledge, not technical capability, must be their starting point when they allocate dollars for development. Their payoff will not come just because they make something better; it will occur only when they have made a product better able to improve customer profitability. Otherwise, it will have little or no value in key account selling.

The initial inquiries that go into technical research and development must be market research. This gives technical people their direction. It brings the market in to them before they invest their fast-fleeting time and talent and in advance of their emotional involvement with a specific method or outcome.

## PRODUCT ENGINEERING

Most products are overengineered. In other words, they are overcosted so that they are overly difficult to sell at high margins or in a manner that can improve customer profit cost-effectively. This is not an argument against quality engineering. It is, instead, an appeal to permit your key customers to influence the type and amount of quality they need by specifying the profit contribution they expect.

Products have two objectives: They must meet minimal performance standards, and they must meet maximum profit-improvement standards. The task of product engineering is to minimize performance requirements and at the same time maximize profit-improvement capability. Exceeding or falling below the minimum performance that can maximize profit contribution is unacceptable management of product development.

Customer standards for improved profit are often far apart from product engineering standards. As with R&D, the customer's standards must be brought into the product engineering process. When "the quality goes in," product development engineers should be able to role play the key account sales representative standing before a top-tier decision maker. What promises are the product engineers enabling the sales representative to make? What dollar values are they enabling him to sell? What product-performance benefits are required to help deliver those values? The answers to these questions will tell the engineers what to build and why.

FINANCE

Consultative Selling is value-based selling. Price is a function of the value of new profits that are brought down to the customer's bottom line. Since value will always differ from customer to customer and from project to project, there can be no standard price list for the product and service systems sold to top-tier customers. The sole generalization that can be made about key account pricing is that it is set to achieve high margins.

Lack of standardization is the bugaboo of corporate controllers and vice-presidents of finance. The world they live in is concerned with improving your own company's profits. Their awareness must be heightened to understand that their mission depends on your mission to improve customer profits. Along with your key account representatives, your costing and pricing people should be taught the Consultative Selling skills and taken into the consultative proposal process, where customer profit improvement is quantified. They can help the quantification procedure. They can also learn how to help your sales force when necessary, either internally or as a member of the sales support team accompanying key account representatives in their customer penetration.

Mobilizing the nonselling functions of R&D, product engineering, and finance on behalf of key account penetration is a tough but necessary task. None of these people are sales people. Many of them abhor sales for its extraversion and extreme people orientation. For similar reasons, they may distrust or demean sales representatives. They may believe that if they "invent it smart, make it good, and price it fair," anyone can sell it. For them, the customer is the last stop in the capital turnover process instead of the first. Science and finance are seen as the sources of profit, sales as the outlet valve, and customer needs are roadblocks in the way of pure science and low-cost marketing.

A key account sales force works with one hand behind its back in such an environment. Only when the people who make your products, cost them, and price them work cooperatively with your key account representatives can selling be planned to bring its full power to bear on key account penetration.

# 4

# Building Multilevel Alliances

## *How to Ensure Customer Partnering*

The process of key account selling begins at the narrow end of a funnel, where a single selling message of improved profit is inserted. It emerges through the wide end custom-tailored to meet the specific needs of each type of customer manager in a key customer's top tier. This contrasts with vendor selling, which originates at the funnel's wide end. A diversity of price and performance specifications are then focused on a single decision maker, the purchaser.

Vendors sell to a homogeneous target, the managers of customer purchasing functions. At their level, the frame of reference for selling is competitive price and performance. At the multiple levels of the top tier, several frames of reference determine whether or not value is perceived and, if so, how much. Key account sales representatives must sell to each of these managerial levels. They must speak its unique language to deliver the same essential message, customizing it so that they can build a sale and, at the same time, structure an ongoing alliance at each level.

76

A key account representative's job can be defined in three ways: bring back sales, bring back new customer information that can lead to sales, and leave behind alliances with top-tier decision makers.

Sometimes a sale will build an alliance. More often alliances help build sales. Because alliances are diverse, they challenge representatives to develop a broad understanding of their customers' business organizations. Because alliances are highly functional, with each level devoted to its own microcosm of the corporate universe, representatives must develop specialization in several customer business operations. These are additional ways of defining what it means to say that every key account representative must "know the customer's business." They cannot achieve this objective without allying themselves with the customer managers who perform the crucial functions of the business into which the representatives sell.

There are four levels on which alliances must be structured in a key customer account. Three of them are in the upper management tier. The fourth is the familiar purchasing level, where the traditional adversary relationship must be converted into a more partnerable affiliation.

## Alliances With Top Management

By selling as a consultant, a key account representative obtains access up and down the entire vertical chain of a customer's organization. This includes the topmost level of chief operating officer, usually the president. If you sell to a division or subsidiary of a large customer company, your top ally may be its general manager. Selling to several divisions, a major division, or to the corporate management level itself will require you to partner at the top at the company level as well as at divisional levels.

Customer presidents will join in alliances with key account representatives if, but only if, their self-interest is engaged. At their level, there are three principal interests:

*1. Financial improvement.* Chief operating officers are preoccupied with the bottom line—profits. They view their businesses as money machines. In their daily routine, they are on the lookout for as many ways as possible to convert investments into superior return. If you can position yourself with them in this context, they can include your sales proposals among their investment options.

Presidents focus on returns. The accountability they have to their various constituencies demands it. Employees, shareholders, directors, and security analysts all lean on them to produce increased profits. Their stake in their presidents, and the presidents' stake in them, put constant pressure on generating improved profitability. In selling to presidents in a consultative manner, you can help relieve some of this pressure. You are representing an added chance to earn new profits if they will ally with you.

*2. People improvement.* Although presidents are fixated on returns, they never lose sight of where returns come from. Profits are made by their people. They are the presidents' prime capital resource. If you can help improve the knowledge, competence, and productivity of strategically placed people, you can ally yourself as a partner in one of the presidents' own major missions.

What can their people learn from you? You improve their ability to reduce the costs of operations so that they will become less of a drain on internal funds, require a lower investment, or be able to return higher profit even from the original investment. You may also be able to improve your customers' ability to enhance sales revenues. If their abilities are upgraded in these vital areas, their profit contributions can be increased and their productivity stepped up by the amount they add to revenues for each dollar of investment in them.

*3. Operational improvement.* All customer operations are cost centers. By their nature, only a few can ever become profit centers. If you can bring down a cost center's investment base by streamlining its operations, consolidating functions, eliminating steps in its processes, or reducing its need for labor, energy, or materials, you can create a natural commonality of interest with customer presidents.

Presidents often ask themselves—and they are often asked by others—"How competitive are we?" By this they mean many things: How good is our product, our people, and our promotion? They also run an ongoing audit of their operations to determine how competitive they are. They call it cost-efficiency. It provides a useful index of just how efficiently their operations are converting a dollar of investment into a dollar of sales or productivity. When you help presidents improve their cost-efficiency, you help them make their own businesses more competitive; that is, you are joining with them to help them maintain their market position, add to it, or regain it. These are always among the most paramount issues confronting decisions at the top tier.

Vendor sales representatives remain largely unaware of the interfaces they could have in common with a customer president. Even if they have the awareness, they lack the ability to implement it so they can form alliances. They are often obsessed with a desire to "get upstairs," which is wrong. The true objective is to be able to form a continuing alliance upstairs so that you can go back again and again—indeed, so that your presence will be regarded as an ongoing added value by customer people at the top.

Because vendors are unable to translate into selling action the common denominators that exist between customer presidents and their suppliers, many of them regard a presidential alliance as a preposterous assumption. In reality, it has a recognizable basis in fact. People at a customer's top tier are immersed every day in selling situations. Everyone from top and middle management levels approaches them with something to sell: a new business venture or new product idea, an expansion of staff or facilities, or a new market penetration. They approach presidents and their committees in a consultative mode. They request the appropriations they seek on the basis of their ability to contribute a superior return.

This is the only way to approach the top, because it is the only way the top approaches investing its funds. When you sell as a consultant, you replicate the approach that is comfortable to customer top decision makers. Vendors, however, ask management to buy on price or performance. Not only is management unskilled in making this type of commitment; it is also uncomfortable at being asked to play a purchasing role. Accordingly, it sends vendors back downstairs.

## Alliances With Financial Management

Customer financial managers, either controllers or financial vice-presidents, share their presidents' criteria for evaluating the desirability of major purchases. They, too, are motivated by return on investment. Forming alliances at their level will require, for the most part, a similar strategy.

Financial managers regard themselves as keepers of the corporate checkbook. In that capacity, they are just as concerned as their top managers about their bank accounts. Even more than presidents, though, they focus on what goes out. They tend to be highly cost-conscious, auditing with exactitude the amounts of investment required to achieve a return as well as the size and nature of the return itself. As the focal points for the corporate struggle for funds, they live with an intimate awareness of the horns of the dilemma posed by any investment situation:

1. What if I make the investment? Will a better one come along tomorrow after I am out of funds?
2. What if I don't make the investment? Suppose a better one does not come along?

It is understandable that controllers are cautious. If they are approached with a vendor's characteristic persuasiveness, their inherent defenses will be heightened. They find a safe haven in numbers—the financial facts of a proposition to buy. Numbers are their words. They speak of reading them, letting the numbers tell them things, and getting their message. In order to partner with them, your representatives will have to talk to them in their own language.

Financial managers are called money managers for good reason. Money is their unit of communication. For them, it talks. It converses with them in terms of its rate of return, its discounted cash flow, and its present value. Financial management is always in the market for money. They want to invest it; to put it to work for their businesses so that it will earn more money, which, in turn, will give them more money to invest; and so on. They are the customer's investment managers. To form alliances with them, your representatives will have to provide them with new investment opportunities in the form of profit proposals.

Controllers and directors of customer financial functions never lack for places to put money to work in their businesses. Opportunities are endless. What they do lack, however, is endless funds. An alliance relevant to them will hardly ever be due to your products or services—unless these can be used in the financial function itself. Your relevance will depend on the new investment dollars you represent and how quickly and dependably they can be obtained.

## Alliances With Functional Management

The managers of customer business functions are surrounded by problems. These are the problems of supervising and administering their operations. They live in a world of people problems, productivity problems, manufacturing problems, quality control problems, inventory control problems, sales problems—whatever their function happens to be, it will have several of these problems as a normal consequence of its day-to-day activities. Business function managers want relief from their problems. They want their attendant costs removed. They want expanded opportunities for greater sales revenues and productivity.

As a result, their principal concerns are to be knowledgeable in three areas:

1. *How to improve their operations.* What options exist for improvement, how they work to deliver

improvement, and what mix of the options will provide the optimal results.

2. *When to improve their operations.* What timing is optimal for the introduction of improvements, how improvements can best be sequenced, and when the payoff from an improvement can be expected.

3. *Where to improve their operations.* What parts of their processes are the best starting points, how their process can be improved most cost-effectively, and where an improvement can next be migrated so that its initial impact can be multiplied.

These principal concerns clarify the reasons why trying to sell functional managers your product or service is unlikely to make a sale. They are unconcerned with products. They care only for how products can affect their operations and when and where to implement them. Their functions are their context for judging what fits and what doesn't, what works and what won't, what is a good buy and what isn't.

The vendor sales approach that says, "I want to sell you something," is meaningless when it is directed to a business function manager. It is, literally, out of context; that is, it has no perceived relation to his function. To say, "I would like to work with you," is equally meaningless. The only approach that makes sense is to adopt the consultative approach and say, "I can help improve your operation, both in performance and in profit." This addresses the business function manager's concept of a problem. It also addresses the function manager in his role of problem solver.

## Alliances With Purchasing Management

The traditional interests of purchasing managers cannot be partnered within consultative alliances. Competitive price-performance considerations are not the consultant's stock-in-trade. Instead, a new set of standards must be introduced into the purchasing relationship to upgrade its areas of concern to the same level as those held by business function managers. Value considerations must replace price. The financial aspects of performance must be substituted for physical, chemical, mechanical, hydraulic, or electronic performance results as buying criteria. Benefits must be recast in dollar terms from the traditional measurements of pounds, gallons, bytes, or man-days.

Alliances with purchasing management have two objectives. The first is to create a consultative partnership that will enable your representatives and their customer purchasers to develop profit-improvement proposals in collaboration with each other. Then, together, they can take them upstairs for joint presentations at the top tier.

The second objective of a purchasing alliance is to develop an implementation exchange. As an outsider, your representatives can help their purchasers by providing access to information and access to higher-level management inside the purchasers' organization, and by educating them in the profit-improvement approach to evaluating proposals. Because the purchasers are insiders, they can help your representatives with internal data on customer needs, decision-making practices, and the politics of functional management relations. In these ways, the basis for an alliance exists.

## Alliance Objectives

The objectives of all key account alliances are similar, regardless of the level at which they are to be achieved. Their goal is to ensure customer continuity. Unless your key account relationships are continuous, there will be no way for you to maximize the profit opportunity that a major customer represents. Unless you can retain your key customers, everything else is academic. You can achieve this goal by following three strategies in your alliances: Collaborate, educate, and negotiate.

*1. Collaborate.* In key account situations, it takes two to make every sale. Your representatives cannot sell alone. Their customer allies must help them sell within the customer's company. On each side, there must be the same dedication, the same commitment, and the same conviction that a sale will add genuine values to both parties. When a sale is finally made, it should be impossible to tell who really made it. This is the test of a true collaboration. The sale is the thing, not the seller.

*2. Educate.* Your organization and your key customers must do more with each other than buy and sell if your relationships are to be continuous. Along with making new dollars, you should both be making new information available to the people on each side who will be collaborating on proposing sales. Not only must you both earn as a result of your relationships; you must both learn as well. Professional growth and personal growth have to attend profit growth.

*3. Negotiate.* The main subject area of the mutual education between collaborators is how to improve profits. This requires continuing back-and-forth dialogue. The flow of inputs must be unimpeded. Suggestions and recommendations must be aired. The ideal environment will be rich in options yet sparse in negative thinking, put-downs, editorializing, or defensiveness against anything that is "not invented here." Free-swinging relationships where there is a high degree of give-and-take help you and your customers to take advantage of important peripheral and futuristic opportunities and cash in fully on solving the problems that are in the forefront of your mutual awareness.

These objectives are easier said than accomplished. They depend on your ability to transform significantly the way you relate to your key account decision makers and their influencers. The result of this transformation is called a partnership.

## Partnership Requirements

Partners are not simply customer decision makers who approve your proposals. Partners are your customer representatives. They counsel your representatives on how to get things done inside their companies, vector them around obstacles, and define the players for them. Partners are your representatives' blockers. They run interference for them, dealing behind the scenes with objectors and foot draggers. Partners are your representatives' anchors. They act as alter egos, their main contact points within the customer companies. Partners are your representatives' version of *Deep Throat,* their news analysts of what is really going on with the customer and what its most probable implications are likely to be.

Partners are your representatives' chief implementers. They are their introducers to top-tier customer managers. They influence other managers to accept your people. They take the major risk of lending their auspices to you, sticking their necks out on your behalf, and putting themselves on the line as testifiers for your ability to improve their companies' profits. In short, partners are indispensable to a consultative relationship. They must be protected as well as cultivated. If you lose a partner, you may very well lose the entire account.

Maintaining partners imposes three requirements:

*1. You must participate.* You must be actively involved with your customers, working closely with them to learn how to help solve their business problems that you can affect. This means more than just proposing and selling. It means finding out when and where they like you to get involved with their problems and then getting into the problems at that point. It means investing upfront time to study their situations, laying down your fact base before proceeding into the selling cycle, and building your acceptance within their organizations on a step-by-step basis.

*2. You must commit.* You must plan a long-term growth relationship with each key account, viewing it as an essential part of your business in the same way you regard guaranteeing critical sources of supply, ensuring your attractiveness to skilled human resources, and controlling your future borrowing power. Your own people and your customer's people must both know your commitment. It should be verbalized in your standards of performance and evidenced in the allocations of your best talent to your key customers.

*3. You must measure.* You must agree with your customer decision makers on criteria for taking periodic readings on how well customer profits are improving. There can be no appreciation of accomplishment without knowledge in advance about how it will be determined. The criteria of performance and profit must be laid down at the start. So must the measurement tools that will be used to read the criteria. Good measuring standards make good partners.

Before a partnership can become operational, and for it to remain in place, three prerequisites must be met. Though few in number they are exceedingly complex for prospective partners to execute.

*1. Mutual objective.* Growth partners must have the same objective: Each must grow the other. The customer's growth, however, is primary. It must be the superior objective of the partnership because it is the drivewheel of the supplier partner's growth. A growing customer will grow his supplier by demanding more growth.

A partnership's foremost growth objectives are always the customer partner's objectives. This makes growth partnering unique as a business relationship. Two companies work for the objective of one. They dedicate themselves to growing the customer partner, who becomes the source of the partnership's wealth.

This is in marked distinction to traditional vendor relationships in which each member is dedicated to its own growth. Instead of acting as partners, suppliers and their customers are adversaries in a win-lose relationship. Each tries to impose its objectives on the other. The customer seeks the lowest cost of goods. The supplier wants the highest margins. If one is to grow, it must be at the expense of the other.

Partners must both win by enhancing each other. Mutual enhancement requires a mutual objective: *Grow the customer first*. Partnerships work because the customer is being grown. They fail when their mutual objective has atomized into "every man for himself."

Customers who have never partnered often find it incredible that a supplier will commit to customer growth. Suppliers who have never partnered often find it impossible to maintain their commitment, lapsing back into moving their products to the foreground, wrapping them in purchase orders, and attaching a price to their features, functions, and benefits. Moving product does not grow the customer. It serves, sells, and stocks but does not grow. Instead, it merely *costs*. Only the new profits of growth will enrich a customer.

*2. Mutual strategy.* Growth partners must agree on strategy—on how the partnership will grow the customer. Each partner must know the role he is expected to play in the partnership. What resources will he contribute? How will they be employed and for how long? Who will manage them? How much will they cost and what trade-offs will have to be made against their allocation to the partnership? Since every resource adds a cost that raises the break-even point of the partnership, a minimal strategy must always prevail.

Knowing how the customer's profit can be improved enables the partners to set up a control system to monitor achievement on a progressive basis. Attaining each milestone "on plan" announces that the partnership is working.

Strategy can be measured—or, for that matter, managed—only if it is explicit. Strategy is not just trying to reduce inventory cost but planning how it will be done: Will labor or materials costs be reduced? Or will insurance costs, security costs, energy costs, or the costs of capital be the expenses brought down? How will that happen? Will materials handling be made more cost-effective or will space requirements be reduced or will turnover be increased? By how much? Within what time frame?

Partners trust each other to the extent that each knows what the other is doing in the partnership. Partners evaluate each other to the extent that each performs according to his role. Partners must do what they are *supposed* to do. This is what is meant by a strategy: taking what is supposed to happen and doing it the way it is supposed to be done.

3. *Mutual risk.* Growth partners must share the risk of partnership. The principal risk is that the partners will fail to achieve mutual growth, the very reason for the partnership's existence. If only minimal growth is realized, the resources allocated to the partnership by both the supplier and the customer will have been squandered. The opportunity represented by the partners' objective will have been lost.

Mutuality of risk means that both partners take a chance on failure. Their risk is unequal. The customer's risk will most likely be greater because the customer, having more to gain by being grown, consequently has more to lose.

## Rules for Structuring Alliances

At all levels of a customer organization, key account partnerships are unusual unions. They are formed in mutual self-interest. They are sustained by adhering to specific rules that help maintain the joint objectives of both partners and, at the same time, advance their individual causes. All the rules conform to common sense. Yet it is not enough to assume that any representative can therefore partner with any customer simply by going about his business or by "being open and aboveboard'' or by ''treating your partner as you your-self would like to be treated.'' Partners must be treated as they themselves like to be treated.

The grandfather rule of partnering is to take a ''we approach.'' What this does not mean is as important as what it means. It does not mean projecting yourself and your own needs onto your partner. ''We'' does not equal ''me plus.'' It does not mean acting in a self-seeking manner and then giving your customer your best regards. It does not mean using the customer, manipulating the customer, or dazzling the customer with buzz words that may distract him from your personal motives.

To be a good ally means displaying actions like these:

1. Add important values to your partners. Supply benefits that are not readily obtainable. Translate them into profit terms.
2. Be a dependable supplier of valuable benefits. Be reliable as an improver of customer profits. Let your partners be able to count on your contribution.
3. Understand your partners' expectations from your relationship and make sure you fulfill them. What your partners receive must be what they expect if they are to go on being your partners.
4. Educate your partners. Help them become more proficient in managing their operations. At the same time, help your partners educate you more efficiently on ways to keep improving their proficiency.
5. Avoid surprises that delay or prevent the achievement of your partnership's objectives. Surprise indicates ineptitude in either your planning or

your implementation. It also implies carelessness and lack of consideration for your partners.
6. Go beyond the responsibilities you have set for yourself. Take extra steps, show extra effort, and provide extra professional or personal benefits.

Partnerships may seem to be made in heaven, but they do not operate there. They do business in the real world, where conflict is inherent in every long-term relationship. A safe form of confrontation must be provided for the partners to work off frustrations—whether these originate inside the partnership or outside its boundaries—to express anxieties, and to test convictions. Devil's advocacy is the safest way of resolving conflict.

You and your customer partners should agree to be each other's devil's advocates. Nothing should be sacred at the idea stage. Why this? Why not that? Why not both? Why either? Add this—what does that do? Take away that—is it an improvement? What can we combine, rearrange, sequence differently, simplify, or enlarge into a superproduct? What can we eliminate entirely?

Devil's advocates sharpen each other, hone their ideas to the most workable few, and keep their partnerships keen, flexible, and stimulating. They give themselves the chance to go after each other in a nonthreatening way. Advocacy is constructive, not destructive. It builds successively on each partner's contributions, adding value as it goes. What emerges is a solution that has been hammered out in the context of the partnership itself. Both partners can subscribe to it because both have participated in its creation. Neither partner can feel ignored or deprived of input. Nor is the end result likely to be the type of compromise that adulterates the expectations of both partners and leaves them feeling deprived instead of enhanced.

## Preventing Departnering

Knowing how to structure partnerships is one-half of the alliance equation. The other half is knowing how to prevent their destruction through the reverse process of departnering.

Departnering occurs when two conditions are met. An alliance that is incomplete or unfulfilled within itself is vulnerable. When a more promising partner appears, it succumbs. Many troubled partnerships linger on because both partners temporarily subscribe to the belief that "You know what you've got, but you don't know what you're going to get." As soon as one partner believes that what he or she is going to get is better, the partnership will end. In key account selling, this means that the customer will be lost.

Because markets are tight communities, the loss of one key customer inevitably raises doubts, creates assumptions, and fosters anxieties that threaten the stability of other key customer relations. A domino effect can follow. The loss of one key partner or one key account will open the door to competitors who, even if they have not been a cause of your departnering, will want to take advantage of its effects. Furthermore, it may be impossible for you to replace the loss over the short term. In many industries, loss of a key piece of business means that you are out of consideration for a next chance for three to five years, when a customer's buying cycle cranks up again.

What leaves an alliance incomplete or causes it to

be unfulfilled? There are two major factors that predispose eventual departnering.

## DIVERGENT OBJECTIVES

Partnerships rest on similar ends. Both partners must have the same end result in mind before they partner, see the same end as being achieved while they are partnering, and be able to look back at the accomplishment of their ends as a consequence of the partnership.

It can be said that partnerships are known by the objectives the partners have in common. The eternal question of what two people see in each other is easily answered: They want to achieve the same objectives, and they perceive the partnership as the optimal means of reaching the objectives. This is their hidden agenda.

A key account partnership is not a one-on-one situation. More accurately, it is a two-for-one relationship. Both partners share one objective—to improve the customer's profit. Unless this is accomplished, the sales representative's other objective of improving his own profit contribution will be impossible to attain. The customer's objective must therefore come first for both of them. This is not philanthropy but enlightened self-interest.

When objectives diverge or simply appear to one of the partners to be going off in different directions or diminishing, alliances atomize. A customer partner may believe that your representative is more interested in self-promotion to the customer's top tier than in merchandising the partnership. The customer partner may feel used, demeaned, and exploited by your representative as a means of furthering your business elsewhere. Your representative, on the other hand, may believe many of the same things about the customer partner.

Whether such perceptions are true or not, they will have an erosive effect on the partnership.

Restating objectives and recommitting to them are essential elements in keeping partnerships on track. Objectives should be brought up for discussion at frequent intervals at the initiative of your representatives, for instance, when progress is being measured against them. At some of these checkpoints, the original objectives may have to be downgraded, or perhaps increased in the event of unexpected progress. Either way, keeping them current will perpetuate their meaningfulness as the end results that both partners are working for.

## UNEQUAL RISK

Partnerships are a means of reducing risk. Two parties can share the load, divide the responsibility, and parcel out the components of the task that would otherwise be borne by one or left undone. While the risk is reduced, it is never eliminated. It must be shared as equally as possible if the partnership is to be preserved. Otherwise, your partner may accuse you of "putting your hand out further than your neck."

No matter how hard your representatives try to balance the risk of failing to improve customer profits, their customers will always be left with the major portion of exposure—inside their own companies; on their own; and on behalf of your representatives, whom they recommend to their people. They are also exposed to their topmost tier of management. In any business situation, there can be no riskier combination of exposures.

There is no question about it: Once customers commit themselves to work with you to improve their profit, they must be successful. It is no wonder that they will be ultrasensitive to their own inherent risk and to the support they receive from your representatives. They have a lot on the line.

Because customers bear the major share of a partnerships' risk, you must take on the major share of reducing the risk and providing reassurance that it has been reduced. You cannot have the same degree of risk as your customers, but you can provide a greater degree of risk calculation and limitation. This must be your equalizer.

You have several equalizing tools at your disposal. One is to be thorough in your fact finding and in putting together the database on customer problems and opportunities. Another is to be diligent in obtaining feedback from your customers about their needs as they express them. A third is to manage your account review sessions with care so that deviations from objectives are caught early when they can be corrected, so that strategies can be revised to meet changed conditions, and so that opportunities can be capitalized when their windows are still open.

Suppose you fail to keep a partnership's objectives from diverging or its risks from being equalized—what then? The result is fairly predictable to forecast. Your customer will seek a new partner who meets two qualifications: A lowered risk and more harmonious objectives. Your partner will also be receptive to a seller who can deliver higher objectives. These may come in the form of greater profits, a more productive product mix, or a broader range of options to choose from in optimizing performance.

Improved objectives may also come from a quicker flow of profits or productivity gains. New monies would come in sooner or existing costs could be reduced in a shorter period of time.

When objectives fall out of harmony, and the inequality of risk becomes uncomfortably oppressive, the emergence of a new partner is inevitable. It invariably is a lengthy process for customers to decide to bite the bullet and open up a search, evaluate possibilities, and then hold their breath while they make a selection. But it always seems sudden to the sales representatives on whom the boom is lowered. Their lack of awareness is the proof of the pudding about how far the partners have drifted apart.

The history of termination of customer-supplier and client-consultant partnerships is filled with surprised suppliers and consultants. "Why, it was only yesterday," they say, "that he was telling me what a great guy I was—how much we had been through together, and how he would always be indebted to me." If it was not "only yesterday," it was "only last week" or "last month." The epitaph is generally the same: "How great it was." Meanwhile, for the new partner, the benediction is "How great it is *going to be*."

## Ensuring Continuity

The ultimate criterion of partnership is that neither partner can afford to let the other partner go. Each is too valuable. Each represents too much profit potential. Each embodies too much of an investment that promises yet unrealized results.

Partners in alliance become invaluable to each other. They are priceless assets, impossible to replicate or replace. Their loss is the equivalent of a catastrophic failure. It is unthinkable.

How can your representatives become this sort of partner and ensure the continuity of their key customer alliances? The following scenario provides the answer.

It is taken from an actual dialogue between a well-partnered customer manager and a would-be usurper of his consultant's role.

USURPER:   I would like to work with you in the privileged position that Phil Smith of the Continental Group now enjoys.

CUSTOMER:   Phil privileges us. That is why he is privileged.

U:   Exactly what does Smith do for you that privileges you so much?

C:   Phil helps us improve our profit more than we can improve it without him—more than we can improve it ourselves—more than we can improve it with anyone else in the functions of our business that he affects.

U:   I can affect those same functions. Our companies are directly competitive. I may be able to improve your profit every bit as much as he does.

C:   But he already is. The best you can say is that you may.

U:   How can I say I can unless you let me try?

C:   I can't let you try until I know you can.

U:   Then how did Smith ever get started with you if he had to prove he could improve your profit before you let him?

C:   That's how. He showed us how much profit he could improve. It was only then that we let him.

U:   I would like to show you how much profit I could improve. Then you would have a choice: Smith's company or mine.

C:   You said you might be able to improve our profit as much as Phil does. In that case, why would we choose between you? In order for us to consider replacing Phil, you would have to do better than he does for us . . . not just the same.

U: How would it be if for every dollar of improved profit that Smith gets for you, I can give you an extra ten cents?

C: That might not be enough to justify our making a change even if you could do it. And you realize that doing it once wouldn't be enough. You'd have to do it consistently. Otherwise we'd be better off with Phil.

U: Well, how much better would be enough for you?

C: Before we could switch from Phil Smith with comfort and conviction, we'd probably have to have someone give us between 50 percent and 100 percent more profit. And again, they would have to do it consistently.

U: All right. Suppose I can do that?

C: How would you go about it?

U: Because we want your business, we'd work harder. We'd be better motivated. We'd work smarter, too. We'd put our best brains against your problems. Besides, we have a better product. Your results would have to be better.

C: But 50 percent to 100 percent better? That's a lot. Even Phil Smith hasn't been able to do that for us.

U: That's the best reason in the world for you to switch.

C: It may be the worst reason. It may be that Phil knows something that you don't know.

U: What's that?

C: Our company. Our business. Our people. Our competitive constraints. In one word—*us*.

Customer continuity can only be ensured by customer knowledge. In the last analysis, it is who you know among top-tier customer decision makers and how much you know about their business operations that gives you insurance against departnering and in favor of lasting alliances. Your interpersonal abilities to penetrate top-tier customer management and the integrity of your customer database are your two principal assets in creating and extending consultative partnerships. Given these, you possess sales-making capacity at high margins. You also possess the partner's positioning that insulates you from competitors' attempts to take you back down to vendor status.

For both you and your customer, alternatives to your alliance must be found wanting. The alternatives must be less improved profit, less shared knowledge about the customer's business, and lessened ability to prepare the customer to meet future industry opportunities with a competitive advantage.

Even in the best of cases, there can be only two possible answers to the question "What is the alternative to our alliance?" One could be another alliance. You must be able to nullify this response by knowing more about your customer's business and being better able to implement your knowledge to help improve customer profits. The other alternative is for the customer to seek remedy internally. You must once again be the better option.

How can you be better than your customers at solving their problems? Your experience and your ability must come into play. Their operating problems are only a part of their business. They are really in business to do something else—manufacture products, for example, and not manage an inventory control system or invest their pension funds. On the other hand, solving one or more of their operating problems is the entire reason for the existence of your business. Their problems bring them costs. Solving them brings you profit. The customers' problems are seen by their people in the single environment of their own business. You see them from the environmental perspective of many companies. You see their similarities and differences, the common denominators of solutions, and the specific attributes that call for customized approaches that are one of a kind.

You key account customers have one overriding need: They must focus on the opportunities of their own business. Problems distract them and detract from the profits that their opportunities provide. If an alliance with you can help free their energies from problems so they can seize their opportunities and seize them more profitably, you have the natural foundation for a partnership in profit improvement.

## The Alliance Contract

Top-tier alliances are implicit contracts. Although they are informal, they are operative because they are based on the mutual self-interest that is the foundation of all partnerships. Alliances are aided and abetted when they are more explicit, especially in their young stages. The Alliance Contract illustrated in Figure 4-1 provides a self-disciplining method for planning and positioning each partnership at a top-tier level.

The contract requires key account sales representatives to define the two focal points that determine a partnership. One is the common objectives on which the allies must agree. The other is the common interests on which the objectives are based. Each of these categories

**Figure 4-1. Alliance contract.**

Customer Decision Maker _____

Position _____

   Will partner with me in an alliance to (common objectives):

     1. _____

     2. _____

     3. _____

   Because of the following areas of mutual importance
(common interests):

     1. _____

     2. _____

     3. _____

should be spelled out in detail, and in quantified dollar
units, on the contract.

A common objective can be to improve the profit
contributed from a customer's operation by 5 percent,
or $100,000, within the next 120 days. The underlying
interests could be to help increase the importance of the
function as a money-maker by $1 million a year in the
plans of top management and thereby make the function
an improved candidate for upgrading and modernization.
These are interests that can be held in unison by both a
sales representative and his customer. The more solidi-
fied a customer partner becomes, the better purchaser
the partner can be. The more contributory a function
becomes, the better prospect it is for further sales that
can yield even greater improvements.

No mention is made in the contract of the sales

representative's self-interests. These would not be shared by the customer. Instead, the representative's interests must be achieved by meeting the customer's needs.

Key account sales representatives should "take out a contract" on every potential ally in top customer management, financial management, and the management of the business functions to which they sell. Contracts have two purposes. This will provide the partners with a platform from which they can work together under the sales representative's leadership. And they will make sure that the representative always remembers his proper position as a profit improver and not as a product supplier.

# 5

# Databasing Sales Opportunities

## *How to Know the Customer's Business*

In key account penetration, your proposals should originate at the same source where they will end—with your customers. They should come out of the customers' businesses first, authentically based on their problems, and then be inserted back into their businesses carrying the added value of your solutions. Key account proposing is closed-circuit proposing. The customer starts and finishes the process. You are the intermediary.

To say the same thing in another way: Profit improvement proposals are born in customer data. From the data, you learn how to qualify and quantify customer problems. You learn the mix of their current solutions. You learn the changes your own solutions can make in customer costs or, as customers refer to it, their allocation of resources. You learn the most receptive entry points to penetrate in order to propose your solutions and partner with the decision makers who stand guard over your entry.

Your key account database speaks for your customers inside your own business. It represents their needs, matches your benefits with their needs, and assigns dollar values to the application of your benefits to their needs. It allows your key account representatives' proposals to come out of the real world of their customer businesses instead of an imaginary world of what your customers "should" or "must" need, want, or desire.

Without access to this kind of customer data, you cannot sell in a consultative manner. Without a way for your sales representatives to use the data in their proposal making, you cannot sell consultatively in the most cost-effective manner.

The relation of Consultative Selling strategies to customer data is a dependent one. Lacking customer knowledge, sales representatives must fall back to being vendors who are forced to sell from the only knowledge they have—namely, price-performance knowledge about their products.

Since consultative selling proposals are entirely dependent on customer data, and since customer data depend on a structure for their accurate, timely, and creative use, a database is required as the centerpiece of your key account penetration.

The database must do more than merely store customer problem and opportunity information and pair it up with your solutions. It must do more than be accessible and retrievable. Structured into a system, it must be able to help your key account representatives generate the proposals that will initiate and broaden your penetration at the top customer tiers of your key accounts. In return, each proposal should develop new information for your database that will provide the basis for additional proposals, and so on in an endless cycle.

## Identifying Top-Tier Entry Points

Entry points into a customer's top tier are provided for you by the existence of business problems that are profitable for you and the customer to solve.

When the job of key account selling is analyzed in its traditional form, most of its total time allocation is normally spent identifying the location of entry points that meet this definition. This part of the sales representative's work is a form of investigative reporting. It involves lining up sources, tracking down leads, checking them out, and then doing heavy-duty spadework. At this point, the sales representative is a long way from standing before a customer, selling.

The next largest expenditure of time is spent internally trying to get the cooperation of his own sales support services: customer service, manufacturing, data processing, credit, financial consultation, and so on. This part of the sales representative's work is a form of legal plea bargaining. It involves negotiation, compromise, and trade-offs of past obligations for present favors. At this point, the sales representative is still a long way from standing before a customer, selling.

Selling, which is the job of your sales representative, takes up the smallest share of their total time.

A key account database* can help reverse the ratio between selling and nonselling time by identifying the most profitable entry points for your representatives at the outset of their penetration planning process. It can also shortcut their time spent on gaining internal coop-

*The key account database scheme discussed here is adapted from Mack Hanan's proprietary APACHE™ database system for accelerated penetration at customer high levels of entry.

eration by quantifying the values of the customer profits they will be able to improve, by providing current credit information on key accounts, and in other similar ways.

Relieved of the up-front delays of entry point identification, your sales representatives can start the selling cycle sooner and thereby shorten its overall length. They can also start it more intelligently. The customer information that goes into a database will generally be the product of many minds, both internal and outside. It will come from the personal experiences of people familiar with the account, from the account itself, from public sources in the customer's industry and the investment community such as *Value Line Surveys, Standard & Poor's Industry Surveys,* and *U.S. Industrial Outlook:* a far wider range of sources than any individual sales representative can ever cover.

A key account database offers more than just information. It offers authentic information. It offers it faster than conventional sources and presents it in such a way that related needs can be combined and comprehensive problems aggregated from them. It offers information in words, numbers, and graphic formats such as computer-generated charts, tables, and diagrams that can be directly incorporated into a profit improvement proposal.

Increasing the amount of time your key account representatives spend before their top-tier decision makers will yield two advantages. By the law of averages, they will sell more and their hits will improve. Second, they will learn more about customer problems from the source of this information, upper and middle customer management. This new knowledge will then be able to fertilize their database to make it even more complete, more authentic, and more productive of sales proposals.

## Structuring the Customer Database

Customer data are live data. Like profits, they are a function of time. In order for the data to be accurate, they must be current. To be useful in proposing improvements in key account profitability, they must be structured in a format that makes them easy to get at and from which it is logical to work.

Customer databases that can act as source materials in creating profit proposals must share the following characteristics:

### INDUSTRY-DEDICATED

If you serve one industry, your database will be dedicated to that industry. If you are organized into market centers, as discussed in Appendix 3, this will be a natural fit. If you serve multiple industries, you must have a separately dedicated database for each industry, just as if it were your only one. In this way, you replicate your customers' perceptions about the peculiarities, the individualities, and the idiosyncrasies of their businesses. You learn to think in the same industry terms that they do, keep alert to the same industry trends and conditions, understand the same industry constraints, and acquire similar industry sensitivities.

### OPERATIONS-CENTERED

If you serve one division or one function of your key customer businesses, the customer and the division or function are synonymous. Your database can be organized along division or functional lines. If you serve multiple types of divisional businesses within your customer organizations, or multiple business functions, your databases will have to be organized by specific lines of business and specific business functions for each customer. The customer is no longer definable as the account as a whole. Instead, "the customer" is actually several individual operations managers, each of whose businesses you must know.

## PROBLEM-ORIENTED

Each customer database must focus on the problems that will be your prime selling targets. These problems will conform to three criteria:

1. *They are important to your customers.* This means that, operationally and financially, they are adversely affecting customer productivity, denying customers added sales, and unnecessarily inflating costs.
2. *They will be profitable for customers to solve.* This means that the total cost of implementing a solution will be less than the continuing cost of tolerating the problem over a "useful life" of three to five years. It also means that the profit from the solution must exceed or at least equal the profit from investing the same dollar resources in comparable alternate ways.
3. *They will be profitable for you to solve.* This means that you can sell the solution at a high margin. It also means that the solution will generate the improved customer profit you have promised so that you will be able to upgrade it and migrate it—and so that you will not have to deplete your margins by providing remedial service, repair, and replacement under warranty.

Into this mix composed of customer industry information, customer operations information, and customer problem information must be added the one element of information that is not derived from the customer: your solutions to the problems in your customer's business functions.

The act of inserting your solutions into a customer database on a problem-by-problem basis unifies your two businesses. It forms the basis for your partnership as problem solvers.

Your solutions should be entered into a customer database in two forms:

1. *Your systems for solving customer problems.* Each product, service, and system you offer should be included as part of your internal information. Its features and benefits should be itemized, together with their symbiotic effects when two or more products or services are combined in a system. Each system should be defined according to its regular and optional component parts. Every offering should be correlated to the customer business functions it affects. Sequential upgrading modules should be itemized so that the contribution of each product or system can be examined from its simplest state through its most comprehensive form. Customer business functions to which the product or system can most naturally migrate should also be specified.

2. *Your system values.* Each product, service, and system should have four values attached to it. The first three are internally known. One is its cost to you. The second is its cost to your customers. The third is its resulting unit margin. The fourth value is external: the dollar value of the costs you can reduce in your customers' businesses or the dollar value of the new sales revenues you can help your customers attain with each

product or system. These four sets of dollar values allow you to know if you are going to be able to meet the two major objectives of every key account sale. One is being certain that your customer will gain improved profit as a result of buying from you. The other is being certain that your own profit will be improved as a result of selling to your customer. If both profits can be improved by a sale, you have the basis for a key account penetration.

Your problem-solving products and their values represent the corollary of your information on your customer's problems and their values. On the surface, it may seem that the products on your side and the dollar values on the customer's side are being exchanged in a key account sale. But your database will remind you that this is not the case. The actual exchange is a transfer of values: your customer's dollar values for your own dollar values. To say the same thing from a customer's point of view, a sale is a trade of a customer's current costs plus the added costs of doing business with you for your near-term and future improvement of customer profits.

## Putting a Database to Work

Dresser-Wayne is a manufacturer and marketer of retail management systems. One of its major lines of business is a single-source system supplied to gasoline retailer chains. It serves major oil company retail outlets and service stations, independent oil service stations, and convenience stores that also market gasoline. Its system consists of gas dispenser pumps, electronic control consoles that operate and monitor the pumps, automatic cash registers, automatic service equipment, and data storage and handling capabilities.

To the individual gas station retailer, the benefits of Dresser-Wayne's system are the timely profit reports on sales that provide the flexibility to change pricing quickly to correspond to peak and off-peak driving hours, accurate cost control, inventory control, and reduced labor. The system also safeguards against downtime and can lower the costs of station design by saving space and increasing the throughput of customer traffic within the smaller space. The retailer's home office benefits, too. It receives data faster and more accurately on sales and inventory. The data can be used to reduce costs and improve sales revenues by allowing improvements in the delivery schedules to each station. In addition, each supervisor at the head office can manage twelve stations instead of six, thereby saving high-priced labor costs at the supervisor level of the chain.

The key account sales force of Dresser-Wayne is equipped with a database for each market segment—the major oil companies, the independents, and the convenience stores. The general benefits that Dresser-Wayne can offer to all three segments are similar: improved profits through increased sales and reduced costs with greater security and control. But the specific benefits vary with the market segment and the problem to be solved. Accordingly, each database is organized to allow each key account sales representative to answer questions like these:

1. Where is the problem at the station level? Is it principally an inventory control problem based on poor cash management? Is it a credit control problem? Are receipts and distribution at the heart of the problem? Or is it a question of labor skills or honesty, quality of maintenance, or the

efficiency of present station design and the resulting efficiency of customer throughput?

2. Where is the problem at the home office level? Is
   it a problem of data control and reporting, cash
   management, or supervisory management?

3. Is this a product sales opportunity, a system-
   selling opportunity, or is there opportunity here
   for the sale of a superproduct composed of several gas pumps, monitoring consoles, a cash
   management control system, data storage and
   handling modems, and a training program?

4. Is this a lease or a buy opportunity?

5. Is there an opportunity to sell a plan to reconstruct individual gas stations to increase traffic,
   or is it more cost-effective to focus on improving
   station profit contribution from existing layouts?

6. What are the total costs to be reduced? What are
   the total sales revenues to be gained? What are
   the investment offsets required to achieve these
   results? What net profit will result to the customer and to us? What is the return on investment?

Each database reports on the total number of outlets
that can be affected in each chain, identifies each one as
being among the top 10 percent, in the middle, or among
"all others," and specifies the average number of gallons
it moves each month along with other products and
services. Data are also included on each station manager's purchase preferences, work force, cost structure,
and use of competitive equipment. Similar information
is also available on home office managers.

Key account sales representatives work with the
type of customer information that is partially shown in
Figures 5-1, 5-2, and 5-3. These three screens are de-

## Figure 5-1. Problem/opportunity summary screen.

Market Segment:   Convenience stores
Customer:   ABC Convenience Stores, Inc.
State/Region:   New York/Northeast

|                              | *Monthly Profit Contribution* |
| ---------------------------- | ----------------------------- |
| Outlet                       |                               |
|   Credit control   | $_____                     |
|   Inventory control | _____                      |
|   Cash control     | _____                      |
|   Staff productivity | _____                     |
|   Maintenance      | _____                      |
|   Throughput efficiency | _____                  |
|   Site layout/size | _____                      |
| Home office                  |                               |
|   Data control and report | _____                |
|   Cash management  | _____                      |
|   Supervisor productivity | _____                |
|   Communications   | _____                      |
| Total contribution/Month     | $_____                     |
| Total contribution/Year      | $_____                     |

**Figure 5-2. Problem analysis screen.**

```
Market segment:   Convenience stores
Customer:   ABC Convenience Stores, Inc.
State/Region:   New York/Northeast
Business function:   Inventory control
Problem:   Stock-out

                                                  Analysis

Average time out of stock                         _____

Number of times out of stock per year            _____

Average number of gallons pumped per hour        _____

Margin per gallon (¢)                             _____
```

voted to the convenience store segment of Dresser-Wayne's market.

On the problem/opportunity summary screen in Figure 5-1, a sales representative has asked the database to show the monthly dollar profit currently being contributed by key functions of stores in the ABC Convenience Stores chain located in New York State. Some of these dollar values will be positive. Others will be negative contributions to profit. The positive values may indicate sales opportunities for Dresser-Wayne if they are lower than average. The negative values may indicate sales opportunities if they can be reduced or eliminated.

The database also tells the sales representative the contributions to profit being made by four functions at the chain's home office. These may provide supplementary sales opportunities.

If the business function of inventory control shows a negative profit contribution or only a small positive

**Figure 5-3.  Benefit analysis screen.**

Market segment:   Convenience stores
Customer:   ABC Convenience Stores, Inc.
State/Region:   New York/Northeast
Business function:   Inventory control

|                           | Benefits |  |
|---------------------------|------------|------------|
|                           | $ Monthly  | $ Weekly   |
| Product loss              |            |            |
|   Leakage       | _____ | _____ |
|   Vapor         | _____ | _____ |
|   Theft         | _____ | _____ |
|   Stock-out     | _____ | _____ |
| Carrying excess inventory | _____ | _____ |

contribution to the chain's profit in Figure 5-1, it can be analyzed as a separate problem area on the screen shown in Figure 5-2. The problem of stock-out can be intensively evaluated according to its gallonage and dollar values. If the sales representative believes these values can be improved, he can create a proposal to compare improved benefits with the current situation. The proposal will resemble Figure 5-3, pointing out the dollar benefits that the representative can bring to the customer on a weekly and monthly basis for any individual store or for the entire ABC chain.

When Dresser-Wayne sales representatives stand before their customers' top-tier decision makers, they hold in their hands a profit-improvement proposal. Its "product" is new profits for the customer.

Dresser-Wayne used to sell ironware: gas pumps

and related equipment. Then its strategy was to sell groups of products and services called systems: not just gas pumps, but control consoles, inventory gauges, automatic cash registers, and data modems with some training and a lease program. Now Dresser-Wayne has transcended products, equipment, and systems to sell a solution: improved customer profitability. It has moved from a "hardware" selling company that did business in iron to a "software" selling company that did business in data to a true retail management company that does business in helping its customers grow their own businesses.

## Monitoring Against Penetration Plans

A customer database can play a dual role in your key account management. It can help improve your profit on sales by increasing the likelihood of presenting optimal solutions to customer problems. In its second role, the database can help you monitor the fulfillment of each sales representative's account penetration plans.

When a customer database has been structured, it can be used to store your plans as well as customer problems and their solutions. Plans will still be prepared in the form of written documents. In addition, though, their major elements can be translated into easily accessible data. At any time, you can call up these data for a performance review across a wide range of subject areas:

1. You can compare the total planned revenues and profits that have been projected by all your penetration plans with actual performance on a monthly, quarterly, or random basis.
2. You can learn the contributions coming to you

from each major industry you serve, to see
whether you are on or off plan.
3. You can evaluate the performance of each key
account representative or team.
4. You can analyze the acceptance of each major
product, service, or system you sell according to
each industry it is sold to, each customer that
buys it, each account team that sells it, and each
problem it solves.

From your performance reviews, you can get a head
start on detecting new areas of opportunity that may be
opening up faster than expected. You can detect trouble
spots before they enlarge. You can alert your key account sales force to the most likely winning strategies as
soon as they become hot and warn them away from
product offerings and sales strategies that seem to be
cooling down. You can apply coaching and counseling
while you can still remedy a situation with more than
just hindsight.

In addition to these day-to-day advantages, there
are also longer-term benefits for you in your role as sales
strategist. By progressively monitoring your achievement against plan, you can begin to collate the success
factors that you will see emerging from your reviews.
You will notice the coincidental association of certain
strategies with results. You will become aware of the
heightened acceptance of certain products, services, or
systems. You will recognize certain patterns and see the
beginnings of trends. Based on your monitoring, you will
be able to create your own personal guidelines to the two
most crucial aspects of key account sales:

1. How to increase the speed of penetration,
thereby condensing the time costs and operating
costs of the sales cycle.

2. How to increase the depth of penetration into high-level decision positions, thereby expanding the number of authoritative information sources who can partner with you.

## Maintaining Account Continuity

Partnerships are dependent on continuity. When one of the partners changes, the partnership becomes at risk. If the customer partner is the one who is being changed, whether by promotion, transfer, or retirement, the effect may be the same as if the customer company itself were changing suppliers. If the sales representative partner is the one who changes, the customer may be open to considering a competitive partner, since a readjustment will be required in any case.

If your key account sales are operated from a customer database, you may be able to reduce the loss of momentum or, at worst, the loss of an account, when one of your representatives moves up or out.

Over the years of a continuing customer relationship, where many changes may have taken place on both sides of an account, the seller's database can be the sole source of continuity. It has a prodigious memory. It never forgets. And it is always ready to teach an account's problems, opportunities, and profit-improvement history to anyone who wants to learn.

Many key account customers take comfort in the knowledge that their supplier partner maintains a database on the problems they have solved together, the business functions that have benefited, the solutions that have delivered the benefits, and the contributions these solutions have made to operating productivity and financial improvement. For many of the same reasons, supplier sales managers take comfort, too.

When you bring into your own business the ongoing knowledge of a customer's industry, the company as a whole, and the problems of the specific business functions you serve, you own an equity in your relationship with the customer. The equity is your ability to maintain a continuous stream of profit-improvement proposals against the customer's operations, free from interruption. The uninterrupted flow of profits from your business is a vital resource. It is the equivalent of a line of credit. Without the certainty that the customer can get it when needed, the value it holds may evaporate. The axiom of prudent business management that undependable money is unspendable money can cause the customer to look elsewhere for a source of ongoing profit improvement.

Every new sales representative who moves onto a key account can be moved first through its database for an automated briefing session. No one needs to take time out for training in the account's principal problems, opportunities, decision-maker propensities, or competitors. The briefing can be repeated as often as necessary or desired. Specific areas of inquiry can be studied intensively. Interrelationships in the data can be creatively cross-referenced.

The same advantages can be made available to new or newly promoted customer partners. They, too, can be briefed by your database to equip them with an early awareness of the values their business has received from your partnership, the types of problems that have been solved together, and the opportunities that still remain on the mutual agenda contained in your account penetration plan.

## Keeping Current on Customer Problems

A customer business is a collection of cost problems and revenue opportunities. Its costs eat away at its revenues. When one cost is reduced or eliminated, another cost is often revealed as the next candidate for cutback. At the same time, the search for new revenues incurs new costs. This creates the need to make sales revenue production more cost-effective. The cycle is endless.

At every point in the cycle of costs-revenues-costs, opportunity is created for the improvement of customer profit by helping to reduce costs and increase sales. This is the basis for key account penetration.

In this context, your sales representatives have twin missions with their customers. One is to penetrate the customer's dollar resources and come back with a maximum contribution by selling something. The other is to penetrate the customer's information resources and come back with a maximum contribution by learning something. What each representative learns will become another input for your database.

Bringing back sales has been the traditional emphasis. Information has been supplementary, amassed informally and regarded as a bonus accompanying the sales transaction. In key account selling, however, information is a coequal objective with every sale. It is the raw material from which new sales will be proposed. Consequently, it is the source of your future profits.

A sale without information leading to subsequent sales is only half a transaction. An installation without knowledge of the values it is contributing and of further problems to be solved is only half an installation. A proposal without insight into follow-on proposals is only half a proposal.

The existence of a customer database provides a

natural repository for attracting current information on a continually updated basis. It gives information a home, acting as a highly visible symbol of the sales representatives' data-gathering responsibility. This responsibility can be integrated into their position descriptions so that standards for performance are met only when they have made customer data deposits of required value during each evaluation period.

Using your database to maintain up-to-date knowledge of customer problems is an organized way to keep yourself "in the market." By allowing the database to pressure you to certify that it is always up-to-date, you ensure your involvement with customer businesses on a close, continuing basis—the best guarantee you can have of being accepted over time as your key accounts' preferred profit improver.

## Accessing Customer Information

Your customer database should become a utility in your key account operations, every bit as central and continuingly useful to them as your other communications utilities. Operationally, the central position of customer data in key account planning means that they are at the pivot point of all your penetration strategy making. Functionally, however, you have a choice. Access to the data themselves may be either centralized or distributed.

In some companies, the database is centralized at headquarters. A corporate or divisional staff is trained to input new data, maintain currency and accuracy for the database, and has sole access to it. Under this arrangement, key account sales representatives are responsible for banking regular deposits of customer information. The central staff, in turn, is responsible for processing requests for proposals from the sales force and delivering them to the sales representatives who have originated the requests. In many cases, a recommended proposal and an optional proposal will be created if an alternative penetration strategy is discovered or felt to be desirable as a standby.

When a customer database is centralized in this manner, the headquarters staff can become proficient in generating profit-improvement proposals. As their skills increase with practice, their ability will also grow to perceive opportunities for standard solutions to recurrent business function problems, to cross-reference solutions from one proposal to another, and to suggest comprehensive supersystems that can solve complex customer problems. At times, the central staff may take on consultative roles in these areas.

Key customer decision makers can be invited to visit the central location to observe their data in the act of being updated or used in proposal generation. Industry sources can attend seminars based on trends and projections in their business segments. The database can become a corporate data center. Architecturally and operationally, it can be made into the solar plexus of your marketing operations. In smaller scale, the same advantages can be located at regional subcenters.

Other companies make full-time allies of key account representatives and their databases. Each representative is equipped with his own terminal, which can be portable or fixed at the representative's local office or at home. In this form of decentralized "buddy system," each representative is responsible for maintaining the accuracy and timeliness of customer information and for using it to create his own proposals.

Given personal access on a twenty-four-hour-day, seven-day-week basis, a representative can be expected to develop an intense appreciation of the value of the database and a high degree of intellectual curiosity in testing the feasibility of new solutions whenever they occur. Since the validity of the representative's proposals clearly depends on adherence to good maintenance procedures, you can generally assume that the database will be well cared for. A small central staff can be made available to help each representative on a demand basis. Simultaneously, they can operate a headquarters installation for top management demonstration and corporate positioning purposes with key account customers and other influential constituencies.

Because key account selling is such a uniquely personal experience between a sales representative, customer decision makers, and the problem-solution information they develop together, there is no substitute for the decentralization of database access to each representative. To the extent that key account representation can be personalized by each person who sells—so that his customer is regarded as "my customer," his database as "my database," and his proposals as "my proposals"— its success can be significantly enhanced.

## Integrating Information and Operations

When you send your key account sales force out into the field, they represent your business to your major customers. You key account database represents your customers inside your own business. If you look at the role of your database in this way, you will be able to see that it fulfills two prime functions:

1. In organizational terms, it is the correlate of your sales force. It acts as the "Mr. Inside" of your customer representation.

2. In operating terms, it is the partner of your sales force. It acts as the "Answerman" of their proposal process.

There is no alternative to a customer database in either of these functions. Nothing else can represent your key accounts so well inside your business. Nothing else can partner so well with your sales force to generate penetration proposals.

In sales management, it is traditional to compare all investment options against the criterion of being able to afford "one more sales representative." In many cases—perhaps most—it might be better to hire the additional representative rather than spend a similar amount of money on something else. There is one exception: If the option can multiply the effectiveness of your present sales force so that you gain the equivalent of additional representatives without having to hire, train, or compensate them. A key account database is exactly such a multiplier. For a start-up investment of somewhere between one and two key account representatives, including their total indirect expense allocations and support service burdens, your customer database can make each of your existing representatives up to several hundredfold more productive.

How can this be so?

Your sales representatives who are equipped with customer information will sell from their information, not from a price list or product catalogue.

They will sell the knowledge of their own business— solution knowledge—in a way that matches their knowledge of the problems in their customer businesses.

They will sell in customer language, which is the language of the financial and operating aspects of customer business functions. Top-tier customer managers speak this langauge and will share it with representatives who speak it also.

Your sales representatives equipped with customer information will sell against customer problems, not against competitors who offer parity products at parity prices. They will defeat their competitors by the superior values of their financial and operating solutions, not on the basis of reduced price. As their values become accepted as the industry standards, the effects of competition on their sales will diminish.

They will sell to customer representatives who want to be sold because they want their problems solved in the most profitable manner. Instead of defending against buying, they will help your representatives sell because it is in their own self-interest to contribute as much as they can to their company's profit.

No one or two additional sales representatives you may hire can have these effects on your current key account sales force.

Any newly hired representatives would be transient. They could leave, receive promotions, or be transferred. Your customer database is permanent. It is an appreciating asset that becomes more valuable over time in the roles of your "Mr. Inside" of customer representation and the "Answerman" for your preparation of proposals. It is always under your control, always accessible, and will never end up working for a competitor.

As key account databasing becomes commonplace for you, customer data will be the No. 2 element in your one-two penetration punch. The No. 1 element will always be the key account representative—the leader of the sales representative-database team. It will be the representative's skill that will add the unique marginal values to the database that endow it with superior usefulness.

A representative can embellish a database with competitive values in several ways:

1. By taking care to stock it regularly, keep it up-to-date, and cross-reference its inputs in varied ways so that they can be integrated into many different types of proposals.
2. By acting ingeniously to test and retest solutions to make certain they are creative, cost-effective, and comprehensive. When the crunch comes in neck-and-neck competitive showdowns, the order will go to the most creative solution: the one that creates the greatest profit for the customer.
3. By searching out the common denominators in successful penetration proposals, recording them in the database in relation to the problems they apply to, and using them as standard frames of reference for future proposals. For many suppliers, as many as 80 percent of the components of successful solutions are repetitive.
4. By motivating customer decision makers to become involved with the representative as partners in the database partnership, so that they can participate in updating its information, adding to it, and developing trust in the representative's penetration proposals.
5. By using database information to counsel with customers on ways to improve their profits even though no opportunity for a sale is in prospect. The periodic gift of something of value without the expectation of compensation is a hallmark of the superior consultative sales representative.

In ways like these, the power of a key account database can be fully harnessed as a sales tool, not just on the merits of its own intrinsic qualities, but supplemented with values added by the person it adds the most to—each key account sales representative.

# 6

# Profiling Business Functions

## *How to Target Customer Operations*

The high margins that accrue from key account selling are your reward for knowing more about the customer operations you affect—and being able to improve them—than your competitors. Margins are merited by mastery of how a customer runs the business functions that are your sales targets. The more you know about them, and the better you are able to implement what you know into proposals for performing them more cost-effectively, the greater your value will be, and the higher the price you will deserve as a result.

Key account selling is industry-dedicated. Within each industry, it is function-specific. Business functions in customer companies are your end users—your true markets. According to the way they operate, they throw off the costs that you can reduce or help do away with them entirely. Business functions in customer companies can add new sales revenues or productivity if you can show their managers how. Their functions are the sources of the problems you will have to solve and the showcases where the value of your solutions will give

129

testimony to your capabilities. Scoping their ways of operating should therefore be your constant preoccupation.

If you are going to sell in a consultative manner, the operations of customer business functions will be the subject matter of your consultation. The only alternative is to talk about your own processes and the products or services they produce. In that case, you will be talking to the purchasing tier, and you will be selling on a basis of competitive performance and price. Your opportunity for high margins will have vanished.

In order to know a customer's business functions from an operating perspective and from the point of view of their financial contribution, you will have to get inside customer businesses. Generic knowledge of a function based on industrywide generalizations is important and useful. But it is insufficient. Industry norms and averages can be extremely helpful, especially if they are used as jumping-off places to learn the specifics of individual customer operations. But by themselves they are insufficient. The actual facts and figures of a competitive company's function may be intriguing and suggestive. But they are insufficient because, as every customer will tell you, "My business is different."

The only business function profile a customer will recognize is its own. It is also the profile the customer guards most zealously, and with good reason. Little perceived value comes from releasing functional operating or cost information. There are many people and organizations that can use it detrimentally. Conversely, there are few if any who might use it helpfully. If you want to qualify as a helpful source, you must first pay your dues. You must do homework on your customer businesses. Then, based on what you have learned and how well you can apply it, you may be invited to propose improvements.

The ability to profile a customer business function is an essential skill to sell at the top tier. In customer functions you will find the problems you will propose to solve. Unless you know the nature of these problems, their importance, their financial values, and the language in which customer top management discusses them, you will be talking to yourself when you get there.

There are four ways to profile a business function that correspond with top-tier management's own ways of scoping it. One is to examine its context within your customer company. The second is to evaluate its operations. The third is to analyze its principal areas of intensiveness: what it depends on the most for its operations. The fourth way is the need to understand a function's decision makers.

## Examining a Function's Context

Every customer operating function is a miniature business. The research and development function is a science laboratory. The product engineering function is a craft workshop. The manufacturing function is a machine shop and assembly line. The sales function is a distribution organization. Each function is tolerated by top-tier management of the parent company because management has decided that owning its capabilities is more cost-effective than buying them from the outside. They all operate at a cost. In some companies, manufacturing is expected to produce a gross margin. Sometimes the information processing function will market portions of its database and bring in revenues. But in general, only the sales function is regularly charged with producing major profits.

Because every business function is a cost center, it has the potential ability of running up expenses that are intolerable—that is, they significantly erode profits. Cost control becomes a paramount consideration with every customer to prevent this from happening. Management thinks of this mission as controlling a function's contribution to cost.

This is the financial context in which customer business functions exist. You must know how these functions fit inside each customer business—that is, how must cost they generate—as if they were your own. From a sales point of view, they are your own: your own market.

## Evaluating a Function's Operations

Business functions are processes. All processes have a flow. They have a beginning, a middle, and an end. Manufacturing begins with raw materials and ends with finished products in inventory. Data processing begins with raw information from many sources and ends with summaries, compilations, and reports. There are costs at both ends. In between, there is nothing but costs.

Every process has its critical few points. There are the places, times, and activities in the course of the process where its major contributions to value are made and where its major costs are incurred. In some operations, these are referred to as choke points. Unless they work in the most cost-effective manner, the output from the entire process may be made cost-ineffective.

You and your representatives should be able to chart the flow of the key customer processes you affect from start to finish. You should be able to assign appropriate costs to the critical few points that control a process and be able to prescribe the optimal remedy for the portion of these costs that you can help reduce or enable your customer to rule out entirely.

Some of your remedies will be therapeutic. They will lower an existing cost. Other remedies will be curative. They will alter a process, combine it with another, or eliminate it from the flow. In still other cases, your remedy will be to change the architecture of a process so radically that a completely new set of cost centers will result.

A process flow is diagramed in Figure 6-1. It shows the flow of activities and the accumulation of their costs in a customer's process from their inception in marketing through the end of the process with delivery and post-delivery support. At each stage, new costs are added.

If the process shown in the figure can be made more productive and therefore more economical by the elimination of only one percent of its current cost, a true monetary advantage can be brought to the customer. Its net effect will be to improve the contribution of profit that can be made by the manufacturing process.

## Analyzing a Function's Intensiveness

All customer business functions are intensive in their use of one or more resources. The sales function is labor-intensive. Research and development is technology-intensive as well as labor-intensive at an extremely costly and highly educated level of labor. Manufacturing may be energy-intensive. Plant construction and equipment modernization are investment-intensive.

The areas in which a function is intensive define the

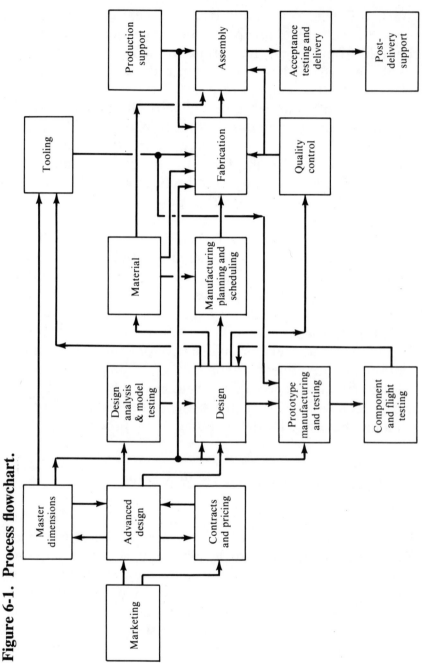

**Figure 6-1. Process flowchart.**

type and volume of its cost configuration. They set the targets for your sales thrust. If a process you affect is labor-intensive, you will want to focus your sales on reducing the amount of labor required, reducing the level of training that is currently required for the work force so that lower-cost labor may be substituted, replacing labor with technology, substituting external contract labor for internal work forces, or improving the productivity of labor so that an additional work force will not have to be hired and each unit of labor can increase its contribution to profit for each dollar of its cost.

In dealing with technology intensivity, electronic controls may contribute more cost-effectiveness than electromechanical or manual controls. On the other hand, increasing the intensivity of labor may be more cost-effective than upgrading a technology.

Your consultative expertise will necessarily fall within the intensive areas of your key customer processes. You will be an assembly process expert for labor-intensive customers and a distribution process expert for sales-intensive customers. In everything you do, however, you must be expert in either reducing a customer's investment intensiveness or increasing his ability to generate a more extensive return.

## Evaluating a Function's Decision Makers

Decision makers preside over every business function as function managers. Influencers reinforce their decisions or argue for contrary determinations. Other decision makers may be found at key steps in the function's processes. Some of them are functionaries. They make a process go. Others are managers. They watch over its cost effectiveness. These are the primary players you must take into consideration when you profile a business function.

Primary players directly affect a function. Outside their circle are the secondary players who are affected by their decisions. These may be primary players in other functions. Taken together, they represent the deciding voices in the acceptance or rejection of your proposals.

You cannot claim to know a customer's business unless you know the decision makers, where they can be found, and where they set their minimum thresholds for making affirmative buying recommendations in your favor. How much improved profit meets each decider's minimum criteria? How shortly must it start flowing in order to be regarded as soon enough? How certain must it be? How much proof is required to be convincing? What kinds of proof are most meaningful?

Only when you know such information about key customer decision makers can you work with them as partners. Only then can you deal with them on a businesslike basis as opposed to simply a buyer-seller relationship. Knowing decision makers means knowing what is decisive for them when it comes time to invest their funds with you.

## Scoping the Options

When you make your initial penetration of targeted customer operations, you already know a good deal about the business functions into which you sell. Even if you have only been vending, you have learned about at least three major subjects. In terms of products and services, you probably understand what has already been done by your key account customers to make their functions more cost-effective. You know what they have purchased, from whom, for how much, and what the results have been.

You also probably know what other companies in your customer's industry have done to solve similar problems. Some of them may be your customers; others may be prospects. From whom they have bought? At what price? With what performance benefits. Third, you undoubtedly know something about upcoming new products and services that might create a difference in customer operations that would far exceed their cost.

Just by being in business, you know most of these things. To be a consultative seller, you must know something more about customer operations. From the outset, you must know the options available for improved customer profits. You will have to study customer business functions so well that you can prescribe the optimal mix of cost-reducing options and value-adding options for each one of their main problems.

1. *Cost-reducing options*. When you screen a business function, you must be able to learn its costs on a before-and-after tabulation. What are its costs right now, today? You must then be able to prescribe the best mix of available solutions that can accomplish some or all of three objectives. They must leave a customer with fewer dollars in costs. They must take a shorter time to reduce costs than other options do. They must be highly certain to succeed.

2. *Value-adding options*. At the same time you screen a customer business for its costs, you should also profile the options for adding new dollar values. How can its revenue-generating operations be strengthened? By how much? How can its productivity be magnified? By how much, and what is the dollar value of the

increase? Here again, you must be able to prescribe the best available mix of solutions that can accomplish these improvements. They must bring a customer more money. They must bring it in a shorter time than other improvements. They must be highly certain to succeed.

There is no such thing as the universal solution. No option to produce less cost for a customer or to add more value will fit all customers, even if the function being penetrated is the same throughout an industry. Essentially, you have two basic choices:

1. *You can combine more value at less cost*—the ideal solution.
2. *You can combine more value even at more cost*— an acceptable solution as long as the added value sufficiently exceeds the added cost.

Either of these options represents good selling strategy. You should have them in mind as you approach a customer operation with the objective of learning its costs and the values it will need from you. By knowing what your options are, you will be better able to select the relevant customer data you need and to structure them to meet your eventual profit-improvement recommendations. In order to come out with what you want, you must go in with the framework of your eventual sales strategy.

## Problem/Solution Definition

A problem that is properly defined is supposed to be two-thirds of the way to solution. The business function problem-definition statement shown in Figure 6-2 is de-

**Figure 6-2.  Business function problem-definition
statement.**

---

Customer/division: ————————————————————————

Line of business: ——————————————————————

Business function: ——————————————————————

Problem qualification

——————————————————————————————————————

——————————————————————————————————————

——————————————————————————————————————

Problem quantification

   Contribution to cost

      1. ————————————  =  $————————

      2. ————————————  =  ————————

      3. ————————————  =  ————————

      4. ————————————  =  ————————

           Total cost          ————————

---

signed to make it necessary to qualify and quantify a
problem in advance of attempting a solution.

The definition statement requires a business function problem to be qualified in narrative terms: what kind
of problem it is for the customer, where it is located in
the customer's operations, what contributions it makes
to costs and performance, and what other problems it is
connected to or is influenced by. Then the statement
asks for an itemization of the dollar contributions of cost
that are currently being made by the problem on an item-

by-item basis. The problem's total cost is summarized as the statement's conclusion.

Figure 6-3 is the follow-on to problem definition. It shows an outline form for the creation of an optimal solution to the customer's problem. It summarizes the problem in descriptive and financial terms and then sketches the essential components of the solution that will deliver the best benefits. The solution outline and the problem statement will form the core of each profit

**Figures 6-3. Solution outline.**

Customer/division_____

Line of business_____

Business function_____

Problem qualification summary_____

_____

Problem quantification total                    $_____

Solution

   1. _____

   2. _____

   3. _____

   4. _____

   5. _____

   6. _____

   7. _____

Total performance improvement                    $_____

improvement proposal that will be developed to make top-tier penetration.

## Profiling a Target Function

To vend, you need to know your own costs. To sell in a consultative manner, you need to know customer function costs. To vend, you need to know your own sales opportunities. To sell as a consultant, you need to know customer sales opportunities. How can you learn a customer's current costs in the business functions that are important to you? How can you get a fix on the customer's unachieved sales potential?

In your profiling of target functions, how can you quantify with reasonable accuracy the operating problems and opportunities that will form the base of your key account penetration plans?

You will need to begin the development of three databases, which will become the basic resources for top-tier selling at key accounts:

1. An *industry* database on each of the industries in which you serve key customers.
2. A *customer* database on each key account customer you serve in an industry.
3. A *customer's customer* database on your key accounts' key accounts.

From your industry database, you will learn the average costs, average profits on sales, average inventories and receivables, and other industry norms that are the standards for its member companies. The information in each of your key customer databases will allow you to compare individual customer performance against industry averages. In categories where a customer falls below the industry norms, you may find sales opportunity.

Your individual customer databases will teach you the concentration and distribution of customer costs. Where do they bunch up? Are these the same places for the industry as a whole? How heavy are they? Are they typical for the industry? What are their trends—are they rising every year or are they coming under control? What variable factors affect them most significantly?

Your customer databases will also provide you with knowledge of where potential new sales opportunities may be found. These may be for improved existing products, new products, combined products, new or enhanced services, superproducts, or systems. How can your customers sell more? How can they sell at higher prices? How can they extend sales into closely adjacent markets? How can they invade new markets that offer superior profit opportunity? How can they anticipate or turn back a competitive thrust?

In order for you to "know your customers' businesses," you must know more than the performance characteristics and cost contributions of the internal business functions that you can affect. You must know the key customers they sell to. They are the customers' opportunity. Their needs are also the determining pressures that cause many of the customers' processes to operate the way they do: to manufacture the kinds of products they make, to advertise and sell the way they do, to communicate inside and outside their businesses with the data and telecommunications technologies they use. Only when you know your customers' customers can you understand the complete spectrum of the consultative relationship that will be available to you—the full range of costs that can be reduced and sales opportunities that can be enlarged.

The essential elements of information you will need to know about your customers' customers are exactly the same as the data you must develop on your customers themselves. You will have to learn the major cost areas your customers affect in their own key account businesses and the main sales opportunities they help these businesses to achieve. Are your customers mainly cost reducers or sales developers for their customers? Do your customers have mature products that you can help them rebrand, as discussed in Appendix 2? Unless your customers have been selling in a consultative manner to their key accounts, it is unlikely they will have customers'-customers types of information. In all probability, they have been vending. They will know their customers' price and performance specifications, their customer decision makers' favorite jokes and luncheon menus, but little else. You will have to learn together what you both need to know.

The joint development of information is one of the strongest bonds for partnering. Joint research can also be cost sharing, another partnering act. At best, your key customers will realize that they will have to expand the knowledge they have of their own customers if they are going to be able to help you help them improve profits. They will, of course, also be able to use customer knowledge to sell consultatively themselves. At worst, you may have to suggest a cooperative starter survey to demonstrate its value.

## Learning From Multiple Industry Sources

Getting into the cost structure of an industry and its customers is a two-stage effort. If you have never done it before, it is a front-end-loaded undertaking. Once you have structured your databases, it is simple and inexpensive to keep them up-to-date. The first stage is to learn as much as you can from the multiple sources that are always available without going to your customers themselves. Then, when you take on the second and third stages that deal specifically with your key accounts, you will have two advantages: You will already know a great amount, so you will have less to ask of customers, and you will have a meaningful framework on which to hang new information they share with you.

In addition to the United States government—especially the Department of Commerce—six additional sources can be turned to for costs and revenue potentials of customers in a key industry:

1. *The people and information resources inside your own company*—the first and most obvious source. Some of your people may have been recruited from customer industries. Some may even have worked for key customers. Others may have participated in market research studies that sought information that can now be related to your needs. If you maintain a library, its periodicals and publications can be culled for data— especially the trade magazines of your key industries. Your librarian can be a valuable aide in obtaining published information of all types.

2. *Trade associations in your customer industries*— staffed by people who usually devote their lifetimes to their trade. They know many generalities and often specific information about individual companies. They know the main leaders in the industry and can introduce you. Their associations also maintain industry libraries and computerized databases.

3. *Security analysts*—professional researchers of

specific industries who are employed by brokerage houses to follow their industries over long periods of time. They publish updated industry analyses that evaluate growth potential, highlight the major factors that determine profits and costs, and define trends that can forecast opportunities. Many analysts will provide personal counsel on a quid pro quo basis.

4. *Industry experts and consultants*—can be retained on a one-shot or periodic basis to lay down a foundation for understanding an industry's process flows and its cost structure. They can also be helpful in estimating the impact of your technology on customer costs and productivity. In addition, they can exchange information on business function problems affecting an industry as a whole and its individual customer companies and the solutions they are currently implementing, or plan to implement, to solve these problems.

5. *Other suppliers*—suppliers of noncompetitive products and services to the same business function decision makers at your key accounts may have acquired knowledge of customer process costs and sales opportunities they will share with you. They will probably approach the knowledge you seek from the bias of their own interests, which may make their information peripheral to your needs. Nonetheless, you may be able to translate it or project it onto the way your own business cuts into customer costs.

6. *Noncustomer companies or non-key account customers in the same industry*—sometimes easier to approach in a quest for general information than your own customers. They operate the same business functions. Their costs tend to cluster in the same critical few choke points. The potential sales opportunities of the industry affect them in the same way as they affect your key accounts. Even though their businesses are different

in many ways from the business of any one of your own key customers, enough clues can generally be found to make their cultivation worthwhile.

## Learning From Public Customer Sources

After you have done your homework with multiple industry information sources and before you approach your key customers themselves, there is an important intermediate step. Every customer company reveals publicly many facts about its existing operations and plans for forthcoming investments or divestitures. These revelations are invaluable to you because they are authentic. They come from the horse's mouth. You should study them, not only as you start up your learning curve in the transition to key account selling but on a continuing basis. There are two major sources from which you can learn what customer companies are proclaiming or complaining about themselves:

1. *Annual reports and 10-K reports* give you access to information on your customers' current financial condition and its trends, their objectives, the major problems and constraints your customers are encountering in achieving these objectives, how and where they are introducing new technologies and systems to alter the intensive nature of their operations, ways and areas where productivity improvement is important, and new product developments and the changes they may make in the market shares of existing products. The annual report is the form this information takes for presentation to shareholders. The 10-K version is far more detailed and far less florid, since it is put together for the Securities and Exchange Commission (SEC).

2. *Presidential speech transcripts* are reprinted in

the *Wall Street Transcript. Forbes, Business Week,* and other business media often interview chief executive officers (CEOs). CEOs appear for interviews on network television and cable programming. The interview format creates a wide-ranging agenda for comment, sometimes eliciting off-the-cuff remarks and spontaneous declarations that can give you important insights. Presidential insights will also provide useful conversational tidbits when you sit down with your customer decision makers in the third stage of your information gathering.

## Learning from Customer Sources

When you have learned as much as you can from industry sources and from sources your key customers make public, then and only then are you ready to confront your customers themselves to learn the rest of what you need to know. By this time, you will have less to ask. You will not have to request anything you do not require. You will be able to phrase your negotiations in "customer language," which is the jargon of each industry. You will be able to initiate discussion by recapitulating what you already know instead of asking for help up front. You will have shown commitment to your customer businesses by your willingness to invest homework time and effort in advance of a payback. And in the course of your studies, many ideas will occur to you for improving customer profit that will provoke further information from their decision makers as you introduce them into your negotiations.

No information source on a customer's business can equal the customer's people themselves. They speak with authority for two reasons. They have the inside track on customer operations; indeed, they originate much of the information themselves. Second, the information they believe is gospel. Right or wrong, their "facts" are the only facts. Their numbers are the only hard, firm numbers. Their concept of costs are the costs you will have to work with. Their view of unfulfilled opportunities are the opportunities you will have to help them seize.

In an ideal world, customer facts and figures would be open to you for your asking. Every now and then it happens in exactly this way. A vendor supplier sits down before the top-tier managers of a key account customer and presents generalized narrative benefits of working together. For the work they will do at the top tier, the supplier proposes a partnership based on Consultative Selling strategies. The supplier reveals minimal customer knowledge and asks to be provided with the rest. The customer somehow senses the value of the benefits and agrees.

The other approach is called the Consultative Selling approach, because it is the strategy that almost always must be used. It is also known as the hard way. It is the usual strategy, because customers do not give internal operating information and its financial implication to vendors—especially to vendor sales representatives. As a result, a vicious circle is set up. A vendor needs inside customer information to switch from vending to top-tier consultation. Yet customers do not release inside information to vendors. Without the information, a vendor will forever remain a vendor. How can the circle be broken?

The only way that experience proves workable is for vendors to first learn as much as possible from industry and public customer sources about customer cost problems and sales opportunities. Then they can adopt a quasi-consultative role as a halfway step between vending and consulting. They share the data they have, offer tentative proposals based on their implications, and thereby motivate customers to share the rest of what they need to know in order to achieve the proposed profits.

In this twilight zone between vending and consulting, vendors are not asking customers to give them information. They are inviting customers to trade information with them the way consultants do with their clients. Trading is acceptable, where giving is not, because trading is rewarded on the spot with a return of equal or greater value.

To make the quasi-consultative approach work on your initial customer profiling, several requirements must be rigidly adhered to:

1. *You must bring something to the party.* You cannot come empty-handed. Your knowledge of a customer's industry and business must show evidence of intelligence and due diligence. Your tentative suggestions for proposals by which customer profits can be improved should demonstrate an appreciation of the customer's rank order of problems and your creativity in solving them.

2. *You must be careful in trying to bend industry generalizations to fit an individual customer's own situation.* Industry norms and averages are useful as points of comparison with a customer's performance. They should never be used to represent the customer's performance. Never use norms from other industries or even from other companies in a customer's industry as if they were customer norms.

3. *You must be honest about what you have not been able to learn and therefore do not know about a customer's business.* When you construct a tentative

proposal, you can leave these areas blank. As a second option, you can insert admittedly soft numbers for assumed cost figures. If you use assumptions, you should try to come as close as possible to your best estimate of what a true figure would be. Then you should deliberately overestimate each customer cost and deliberately underestimate the value of your solutions.

4. *In your trial proposals, you must be able to show dollar benefits for a customer manager that meet his threshold of what is significant.* Unless you can do this, the customer will have no incentive to trade information with you. Partnering must promise a clear reward. The customer must believe it to be achievable by working with you and must also be able to visualize continuing the relationship after the first success.

5. *You must make it simple for a customer to agree to trade business knowledge with you.* This means that you should require as little information as possible. It also means that you should not require any information that a customer knows is publicly available about his business. You should not ask for major allocations of customer resources to further your work together. Your partnering requests should involve the fewest possible customer people, time, and expense.

6. *You must believe that you can improve a customer's profit to the extent you claim.* Your conviction will be contagious. It will be tested by customer decision makers who have never worked with you before—or with any supplier—in a consultative manner. Their comfort level in going ahead will be reinforced by the assurance you convey and the degree of support from your own resources that you are willing to commit.

## Asking for Rights Before Proving Rewards

The quasi-consultative approach proposes a probable reward, shows the size of the up-front investment to arrive at it, and asks for a customer contribution of knowledge to firm up the exact dimensions of the reward. Sometimes vendors try a shortcut. They lack the unique human resources to create a consultative partnership from a standing start. They also lack the dedication to do sufficient homework, or perhaps they feel they do not have adequate skills or time to first study customer industries and businesses on their own. Their approach is to ask customers for the right to study their businesses on the chance that ways and means of improving profits will be found.

Regardless of how customers respond to this approach—and customers occasionally react with favor, especially smaller companies who have not had their operations already studied to a fare-thee-well—it demeans suppliers. It depositions them from any pretension of being expert. It fixes suppliers at the level of graduate students performing summer internships.

There are two principal risks to asking for the right to make a study before proving or even suggesting a reward. One is that studies that begin from ground zero range unnecessarily wide in search of targets. This involves many customer people, interrupting their work and increasing the chance that more than a few of them will be inconvenienced or antagonized. Some may refuse to participate. Others may think the approach is naive. These are frequently the same people who will have to be partnered with if a consultative relationship is eventually established. It is not likely they will readily perceive the vendor as an equal, let alone an expert.

The second risk is that even good results from such studies will be downgraded by the customers' top-management tier. The most typical criticism is "All they told us is what we told them." Since customers know they have provided all the information that goes into a study, they regard the database that results as their possession.

There is no sense of participation in its evolution. As a result, there is no felt need to reward the vendor for what customers believe they themselves have done for the vendor—rather than the other way around.

Asking for the right to study a customer's operations should be a last resort. It should never be a strategy of first choice. When a study is undertaken, it should be minimally disruptive and tightly managed for limited objectives to supplement what you already know. It should also be extremely short.

## Managing Your Business Function Knowledge

The phasing of your emergent expertise in the business functions you affect in key customer accounts will probably take place in this type of sequence:

1. You will know a little about one function in one customer company in one industry.
2. You will know a lot about that one function in that customer company.
3. You will know a little about another function in the same customer company, because you will be invited to migrate your profit-improvement strategy to another aspect of the same business function or to another function that you can affect.
4. You will know a little about the same function in a second customer company, as you penetrate other key accounts in the same industry.
5. You will know a lot about that same function in several customer companies. You will be storing their facts and figures in your databases. Your

expertise in bringing profit improvement to the function will spread throughout the industry.

6. You will acquire similar databases and expertise for improving the profit contribution of other functions in the same business and throughout the industry.

7. You will extend your knowledge and repute to other industries.

This is the capsule history of how major corporations manage their customer knowledge, extending it from operation to operation within a business function, then to other business functions, then to other customer companies in the same industry, and then to other industries. In order to grow their key account sales at high margins, they have marketed their knowledge of customer business problems and opportunities. On the surface, they have been selling profit-improving solutions. But the underlying value has been their understanding of customer problems. They appear as solution experts. At rock bottom, however, they are process-smart, operations-smart, function-smart—that is,—customer-smart. Only then can they be smart suppliers.

As you learn how to manage your customer knowledge resources, you will discover two truths. No customer wants to be first with anything new. Yet as soon as something new produces superior results, every customer wants to retain you to implement the same development with it on an exclusive basis. These paradoxical attitudes will be reflected as you take the first steps from vending to Consultative Selling. Finding the first customer to work with—to let you inside heretofore proprietary operations—will be more difficult than finding the second. Yet working with a second customer in the same industry may also be difficult, because the first customer will want to monopolize your function-profiling skills and profit-improving strategies.

In spite of these initial constraints, you will know you have achieved consultant recognition in a customer industry when a remarkable event occurs. You will be invited by customers to profile their business functions—not to make a bid, but to study a customer's cost structure or sales opportunity. At that point, your knowledge of your own norms—the values you can add to a customer—will come importantly into play. Once you have captured the knowledge of their processes, your proposals for improvement will follow naturally. After all, who will be better equipped?

What you know about customer functions will not be the sum and substance of what you sell. But what you sell will always be based on what you know.

In many sales organizations, realization is accompanied by pain as the balance of power swings from products and pricing specialists to customer operations specialists as they move to selling to the top-tier management of their key accounts. Product knowledge will always be preeminent at the vendor's purchasing tier. But a sales organization will be permanently welded into position there until it acquires the customer data that enable it to move up. The short-run agonies of change must be balanced against the long-term agonies of decreasing margins, increasing competitive parity, and rising costs that can never be retrieved by price. The difference between top margins at the top tier and eroding margins at the purchasing tier is in what you know and who you know in your key accounts.

# 7

# Planning Account Penetration

## *How to Maximize Customer Contribution*

Your key customer accounts are your single most precious resource. Nothing rivals their importance. They are your major source of profits. They are the major source of needs to which your technology, your product development and engineering, your manufacturing, and your marketing must respond. They are, in short, your core market.

Each key account is vital as a profit contributor. Opportunities you fail to serve in a key account are the most unaffordable losses you can suffer. The loss may be in more than profit. The entire account may be lost if a competitor can serve it better. On a short-term basis, the loss of a major customer is irreplaceable. In some industries where it may take five years or more to get back in the ball game, any loss becomes long-term. Meanwhile, all the potential upgrading and migration sales that could have flowed from your original penetration are forsaken as well.

The defection of a key customer, or the abdication

on your part of the opportunity to serve a key customer more comprehensively, is unsupportable. You should therefore treat every key account as if it were a market unto itself. You should analyze its problems and opportunities, quantify its contribution to you and your contribution to it through the sales of your solutions, and position yourself as one of its most significant profit improvers through a personalized key account penetration plan.

A penetration plan is your annual blueprint for getting into and staying in the business of a principal customer. The way you get in is by improving the customer's profit. The way you stay in is by continuing the customer's profit improvement, extending it to the solution of new problems, and never letting go. Last year's profit improver who has let go is last year's supplier of choice.

The account penetration planning process requires you to answer the three critical questions that can determine up to 80 percent of your profitability on sales:

1. Who is my customer?
2. What can I do to improve my customer's profit?
3. What will my customer do for me in return?

The answer to the first question is crucial. Your customer is never a customer company as a whole, nor is it a customer division or business unit. It is a specific business function manager whose costs you can reduce or whose contribution to sales you can increase. If you are IBM, your customer is not PepsiCo. Nor is it PepsiCo's Frito-Lay division. It is the manager of Frito-Lay's inventory control function, for example, whose profit contribution you will be improving.

Similarly, if you are AT&T, your customer is not

Merrill Lynch or, within it, the Diversified Financial Services division. Nor is it the division's real estate management functions. Your penetration plan would be directed to the division. But the business function manager in real estate telemarketing is your customer. It is the manager's profit contribution you will be improving. If you are General Foods, your customer is not Grand Union supermarkets. It is the dry cereal department management group throughout the chain.

Planning to penetrate business functions within divisions or departments of customer companies is a far cry from vending commodity merchandise to purchasing managers on a price-performance basis. It is a totally different business. It must be sold in a different manner. It must therefore be planned in its own way.

## Planning High-Penetration Objectives

Key account penetration planning hinges on one central concept: maximizing contribution. Two kinds of contribution are involved. One is your profit contribution to a customer. You must maximize it. The other is a customer's profit contribution to you. You must maximize it also. This defines your prime objective in key account penetration. You will have to be a maximizer of profits.

To be a profit maximizer is a different role than acting as a need analyst or a benefit provider or a problem solver. All of these are intermediary steps. The ultimate step is that through needs analysis, the provision of benefits, and the solving of problems, profits become improved. Unless this takes place, all the intermediate objectives will be in vain.

High penetration objectives—objectives for your customer's top tier and for you as well—are financial objectives. Nothing supersedes them. They must come first in your penetration plan, because they are the purpose of the plan. The only reason to plan is to be able to set and achieve high financial objectives.

Your plan's objectives should be stated in the following manner:

1. The most likely profit contribution that will be made *by us* to the customer.
2. As a result, the most likely profit contribution that will be made *to us* by the customer.

"Most likely" profits are a conservative estimate that is more bullish than bearish. They represent the contributions that can be expected if most strategies work according to plan, and if there are no important hitches that have not been planned for. In practice, they should come out just about right.

If you help customers improve their profits from incremental sales, you will have to adjust the gross profits they make before taxes by the customers' effective tax rate before you commit to an objective. If you improve customer profits by saving or eliminating costs that can flow directly to the bottom line, you can calculate their profits as net incremental gain. Only the net counts. Neither you nor your customers can take anything else to the bank and draw dollar for dollar from it.

The total gross contribution you expect to make to your customers will be the sum of all the profit improvement proposals you plan to fulfill or partially fulfill in their business functions during the year. The contribution you plan for your customers to make to you will be the sum of your profits from the sale of each proposal that are collectible during the same year. To help keep track of how effectively your key account teams are managing the allocation of their resources to obtain each customer's contribution, you may want to monitor two ratios. One compares profits to the expenditures required to achieve them. This is a form of return on investment. The second is the more traditional ratio of your revenues to expenses.

## Planning a High-Penetration Strategy Mix

Objectives are a plan's purpose. Strategies are the plan's methods of achieving its purpose. In key account penetration, a plan's strategies are contained in its accompanying profit-improvement proposals. Each proposal represents a strategy to improve customer profits by solving a cost or sales problem. If the customer is a not-for-profit organization, or a government agency or department, your proposal strategies will have to reduce costs and improve the dollar value of productivity. Whether your customer is a public corporation or a government agency, your mix of strategies will need to make a measurable impact on customer performance.

Profit-improvement proposals are the delivery vehicles for your penetration strategies. They are designed to penetrate the customer's business as high-level points of entry. Each proposal contains a strategy for solving a specific customer problem. The strategy will be composed of a package of your products and services called a system. All your proposals taken together for the period of a year constitute your annual strategy mix for a customer. There are three steps to take before you propose profit improvement.

ANALYZING A CUSTOMER'S BUSINESS POSITION

Every customer division whose functions you affect occupies a position on the life-cycle curve. If you define that position, understand its implications for your penetration strategy, and structure your profit improvement proposals in accord with it, you can significantly add to their hit ratio.

There are three customer business positions that have a determining effect on your strategy mix. They are growth, the stable position, and maturity. Each one presents a different penetration challenge.

1. *Penetrating a growth customer.* A growth customer is sales-driven. If you want to affect the sales function, you must increase its productivity so that it will be able to generate more profits per sale or to yield added profits from incremental sales. If you cannot affect sales, but instead your impact on a customer's business is to reduce costs, the saving you achieve for the customer can be applied to support more sales. Your entire penetration strategy must focus on improving the customer's profits by increasing sales.

2. *Penetrating a stable customer.* A stable customer is driven from two directions at once. Sales must be increased, but not if this requires increased costs. If projected sales fail to result, the customer's stability can be threatened. Costs must be reduced, but not at the risk of reducing sales or market share. If sales fall, the customer's stability can be threatened. Your penetration strategy can focus on improving profit through sales increases or cost decreases, but it must avoid the risk of increasing costs or decreasing sales in the process.

3. *Penetrating a mature customer.* A mature customer is cost-driven. If you can help lower or eliminate a cost, you can often help improve profit on a dollar-for-dollar basis. The dollars the customer needs to slow the loss of market position will mostly have to come from funds reclaimed from costs. They are unlikely to be

appropriated by management. As a result, your penetration strategy must focus on making the customer's cost structure relinquish money for use in growing the business.

## POSITIONING YOUR PENETRATION STRATEGIES

The purpose of analyzing a customer's business position is to be able to custom-tailor your penetration. If a customer is growing, you must present yourself as an improver of profit on sales. If the customer is stable, you must present yourself as a profit improver by increasing sales or profits per sale on the one hand and, on the other, by decreasing costs. For a mature customer, you must present yourself as being a profit improver primarily through cost reduction.

Unless your position coincides with the customer's, you will never be able to create a partnership in profit improvement. The customer will not understand where you are coming from in your proposals. You, in turn, lacking a sense of your customer's objectives, will not know where the customer is going. As two unknowns, you will be talking past each other; you will be proposing to yourself.

To ensure that your position is in gear with your customer, your penetration strategy should be preceded by a positioning statement. The statement ought to contain three references: your position with reference to the customer, the customer's position on the life-cycle curve, and the general strategic directions you will adopt. A model statement reads as follows:

"In our penetration of the manufacturing functions of the ABC Company's XYZ Division, a stable business, we will position ourselves as the manufacturing vice-president's partner in profit improvement primarily by

means of the reductions in costs we can deliver through-
our quality control system. We will also show how
enhanced product quality can further improve profits
through incremental sales.''

## PINPOINTING PENETRATION OPPORTUNITIES

When a customer is unable to bring down a cost or to
increase profitable sales volume, major business problems result, which may be penetration opportunities. In
order to find out, you will have to identify the problems
and then put dollar values on them and on the most cost-
effective solutions you can devise to counteract them.
This is the information that should be loaded into your
key account database. Your sales representatives will
need it to develop their profit-improvement proposals.

Opportunities to penetrate a key account have a
special genesis. A penetration opportunity does not automatically come into being simply because a customer
has a problem and you happen to have a solution for it.
Discovery is not opportunity. A penetration opportunity
is determined by an analysis of three values:

1. *The dollar value of the customer's problem.* How
   significant is it? Is it making a significant negative
   contribution to customer profit? Does it justify a
   significant expenditure for solution?
2. *The dollar values of the profits from your solution*
   that will accrue both to you and to the customer.
   How significant are they? When will they begin
   to flow? How long before their total amount
   finally accrues?
3. *The dollar values of the costs of your solution*
   that will be incurred both by you and by the
   customer. How significant are they? Are they all

up-front or can some of them be paid for out of the solution's improved profits?

Penetration opportunities are entry points. You should regard them as windows. An opportunity window is fleeting. It never remains open very long. Entering it first is very important. Entering it with the best solution is even more so.

## Proposing Profit Improvement

Profit-improvement proposals are the basic sales tools for key account penetration. They are designed to penetrate at high customer levels and to sell at high-profit margins. Frequently they are crafted for specific high-level decision makers to reflect their functional or personal perspective on the customer problem you are proposing to solve. In all cases, they identify you as a service business that can affect the financial state of the customer's business—the fundamental consultative positioning for key account penetration. There are three types of profit-improvement proposals:

1. *Entry proposals.* When you penetrate a customer's business for the first time or penetrate a new business function within the same customer account, you should construct a proposal that will guarantee successful entry. First proposals must deliver. For this reason, they should be conservative in the amounts of improved profit they promise and in the time frames they allow for the profit's inflow. A safe rule is to "promise less profit and allow more time." Showing speedy results is the paramount consideration: demonstrating to the customer that profit can be improved and doing so in the

shortest possible time. This dictates that you should select an entry problem whose scope you can limit and whose forthcoming solution you can vouch for at the highest level of confidence.

2. *Mainstay proposals.* Your core strategies for customer penetration are the mainstays of your annual penetration plan. These are your bread-and-butter proposals that are designed to solve comprehensive customer problems and deliver major amounts of profits to both of you. As a group, they should yield about 80 percent of your annual profit contribution to each account and a similar proportion of each account's contribution to you. When this occurs, you will know that you are managing your key accounts "according to plan."

3. *Opportunity proposals.* No matter how well you plan, opportunities will rise up in the course of your progressive penetration of each customer. The solution of one problem almost always reveals another. The success of one solution almost always provokes interest in another application somewhere else.

As your customer database grows, more opportunities to propose will become available. Even though you have not planned them, you should keep on your toes for the chance occurrences that invite a proposal. When they come, you can structure a solution for them. Some of these opportunities will be entry proposals. Others can turn into mainstay proposals. that open up entire new areas of profitability for you and your customers.

All three types of proposing need to take into consideration four guidelines: Follow the proper sequence for the proposal, justify high margins, partner with top-tier decision makers to implement the proposal, and migrate initial sales success.

## SEQUENCING THE PROPOSAL

A profit-improvement proposal follows a logical sequence. It begins with a definition of the operating and
financial aspects of the customer problem you are proposing to solve. From there, it defines your solution in
terms of the operating and financial benefits. It then
specifies the dollar differences between the solution and
the problem. This is the profit that will bring improvement to the customer's current situation.

The proposal's purpose is to move your goods. Yet
as much as 90 percent of its content will be devoted to
information about what you can do financially for a
customer's business rather than what your products and
services can do in terms of performance benefits.

The remaining 10 percent of information will be
composed of business function operating information
that the customer already knows and that you must
know, too, in order to help improve profit. These facts
must have a permanent home. There is no better place
for them than your key account database.

A profit-improvement proposal is solution-driven,
problem-oriented, and profit-centered. Customer problems must be presented in the context of their effect on
profits. Your solutions must be presented in the same
context.

Vendor proposals are based on competitive claims
supported by specifications. Consultative proposals are
contrasts between two types of information: what a
customer's managers know about their own business,
and what you know about bringing improved profit to it.
Competitive comparisons are totally absent. Specifications of products, services, or systems go into an appendix.

## JUSTIFYING HIGH MARGINS

The dollar value of the cost incurred by a customer to obtain your solution is your price. If you were selling to a customer's bottom tier in the manner of a vendor, your price would be based on a resolution of your costs and fair market value—the prices being charged by your major competitors. This would guarantee you low margins.

The end objective of key account selling is to obtain high margins. To do so, you must free price from cost and competitive pricing points. The dollar value that a key account customer pays will be higher than vendor prices only if you base them on the profit dollars that your proposal calculates will be generated by your solution. The greater the extent to which you improve customer profit, the greater justification you can have for demanding a high-margin price.

Consultative pricing is value-based pricing. The value it is based on is the dollar value of the customer profits that are derived from your solution. Your incentive to supply high amounts of improved profits to your key accounts is built into your pricing policy. In this way, your individual objectives come together as one. You both want the highest possible profits to accrue to the customer. Added profit dollars are essential to capitalize business growth. The customer must have improved profits in order to justify paying your margins and to be motivated to buy from you again.

Unlike vendor selling, where price is the central haggling point—the customer wants the lowest price while the vendor wants the highest—profits are the issue in consultative sales. Both parties want them to be high. With this powerful mutual objective at the heart of your consultative relationships, a natural incentive exists on both sides to form close continuing partnerships.

## PARTNERING WITH TOP-TIER DECISION MAKERS

Vendors and their customers enjoy adversary relationships. Vendors "overcome customer objections," say "yes . . . but" a lot, and routinely force trial closes on customers who, at the same time, are defending themselves with equal artifice and guile. Consultative sales relationships are very different. The sellers learn as much as they can about customer business problems that they can affect, study the current contribution they make to customer profits, and propose how they can improve the contribution. Since their customers spend their working days doing the exact same things, consultative sellers and their customers work in parallel instead of on a collision course.

People who work in parallel can work as partners. Selling partners play consultative roles. Buying partners become clients. Clients are not just customers with feathers. They are customers who share common objectives with their consultants. As a result of sharing these common objectives, there is no "yours" or "mine." A single set of purposes is blended. Both partners are dedicated to the partnership because neither can benefit as well in any other way. The key word between partners becomes "we."

Partners conduct their business in distinctive ways. They provide easy access to each other, no matter how high their levels or what their disparities may be. They share information with each other. Principally, the information is about the customer's business, because no profit improvement is possible without a database of problems and penetration opportunities. They exchange

speculation about solutions to problems in the customer's business in a manner that is free from the pressure
of early commitment or self-serving foreclosure of the
dialogue, even on a trial-close basis. Once they achieve
results together, they tend to shut out competitors for
each other's time, information, and resources.

From a customer's point of view, your key account
sales representative and support team serve as dedicated
resources that know about the customer's profit situation
and can improve it. From your key account representative's point of view, customers are dedicated resources,
too. Customers provide knowledge of prime penetration
opportunities. They provide the counsel of their decision
makers and their influencers on a confidential basis,
further revealing their business needs. They provide
profitable sales and potentially endless migrations of
initial sales into fresh areas of implementation.

## Migrating Initial Sales

Key account penetration is a reciprocal process. Preliminary partnering makes initial entry possible at top-tier
levels. Once entry has been accomplished, partnering
should proceed apace so that migration opportunities
open up beyond the initial sale. The purpose of preliminary partnering is to gain entry. The purpose of entry is
to migrate, to penetrate a customer business in breadth
and depth.

In addition to the obvious benefit of providing you
with ongoing high-margin sales opportunities, migration
offers several other advantages. It helps amortize the
cost of your original penetration investments for sales
team training and data collection. It helps develop new
information sources about a customer business. It
spreads awareness of your consultative positioning. And

it helps you deny opportunistic chances for your competitors to move in on profitable problems that you can, and should, solve.

Some migrations occur naturally. The solution of one problem leads progressively to the discovery of another. Or a solution in one division of a customer business stimulates internal interest about its transfer to a similar functional problem in another division. Other migrations take place only as a result of effort. You will have to search out opportunities in the nooks and crannies of your customer businesses, relying on your partners to counsel you about the most productive areas to explore and to point out the most cooperative guides to ask for advice.

The objective of penetrating a customer business in depth is to serve all major needs with your major products, services, or systems. This concept can be called maximizing "share of customer" as long as you understand that it is not simply a volume criterion, but a standard of the importance of your involvement. If you are significantly involved, you can become the preferred supplier for your customers' major needs. Penetration in depth is inextricably tied to penetration in important areas of a business. Migration must be a selective policy whose aim is to consolidate your position as profit improver of the most vital functions you can affect.

The ideal migration timetable makes improving profit in one function the jumping-off place for the next one. In this way, you can extract maximum learning value from each experience. You can also avoid stretching your resources too thin across more assignments than you can handle. It pays to remember that migration works both ways. One significant success encourages permission to try another. One significant failure discourages permission to try anything more at all.

## Optimizing the Customer's Mix

Before a key customer becomes a partner, and you are still faced with the problem of making your initial penetration, your choice of entry strategy can be critical. It can determine your rate of penetration, the perceived professionalism of your claim to consultative positioning, and in many cases, whether or not you penetrate at all. By thinking of the customer's current way of managing a business function as consisting of a "mix" of various suppliers' products and services and then offering to optimize the mix—that is, help it deliver its optimal contribution to profit—you may be able to make penetration where all other strategies will be rebuffed.

Every customer has allocated certain resources to each function. Some of these resources are supplied internally: the customer's own people and the processes they perform. The remaining resources come from outside: products, services, and systems that have been integrated from a variety of suppliers. Taken together, these internal and external resources are the customer's current operating "mix." If you want to penetrate it, you will have to improve the ability of the mix to contribute higher profits or greater productivity. There are three ways you can accomplish this objective:

1. *You can supplant one or more elements in the current mix*. If the mix is labor-intensive, you may be able to reduce its cost by substituting an automated process or eliminating an operation altogether. Or you may be able to combine multiple processes in a customer's sales function into a network, such as forecasting and inventory control, eliminating overlapping or duplicated costs.

2. *You can substitute your product or process for a competitive product or process that is part of the current mix.* The basis for your recommendation must be that improved financial benefits will accrue to the altered mix—not simply that more advantageous performance benefits will be realized.

3. *You can restructure the mix in such a significant manner that you will be the sole knowledgeable expert in its revamped composition, operation, and contribution to improved profit.* Your identification as the sole source, or at least the originating source, of a new functional approach can help pull through your penetration as well as make it easier to push. In addition to the improvement in profits you bring about, the prestige of working with the industry innovator may provide extra motivation for customers to become partners with you.

The specific tactics of penetrating by means of optimizing a customer's mix will depend on the industry you serve.

If you sell personal care products to major supermarket and drug chains, you can penetrate by optimizing the mix of their current displays in terms of the number of facings they allocate to your products and competitors', the location of your facings, and the type of displays. The proof of your optimization will have to be quantified in financial and operating benefits, such as profit improvement per square or linear foot, overall improvement in the personal care department contribution per store, or improved profit contribution from related-item sales.

If you sell financial services like stocks and bonds, insurance, real estate investments, or money market funds to affluent individuals, you can penetrate by optimizing the mix of their current portfolios in terms of

growth potential, risk, and current payout. The proof of
your optimization will have to be quantified in dollar
benefits such as higher earnings, lowered taxes, or increased net worth.

Figures 7-1 through 7-5 show how a sales representative who sells scientific instruments can help optimize
the mix of a hospital laboratory.

In Figures 7-1 and 7-2, the sales representative uses

**Figure 7-1. Equipment configuration analysis: present
mix.**

|  | Number per Year | Price | Annual Cost |
|---|---|---|---|
| Equipment |  |  |  |
| Instrument A | _____ | _____ | _____ |
| Instrument B | _____ | _____ | _____ |
| Instrument C | _____ | _____ | _____ |
| Instrument D | _____ | _____ | _____ |
| Accessory Sets |  |  |  |
| Set 1 | _____ | _____ | _____ |
| Set 2 | _____ | _____ | _____ |
| Set 3 | _____ | _____ | _____ |
| Set 4 | _____ | _____ | _____ |
| Materials |  |  |  |
| Material XX | _____ | _____ | _____ |
| Material YY | _____ | _____ | _____ |
| Material ZZ | _____ | _____ | _____ |

**Figure 7-2. Financial analysis: present mix.**

Depreciation

    Total annual instrument depreciation $ _____
    (Total # instruments × average price/useful life)

Lease Cost

    Total annual instrument lease cost $ _____
    (Total # leased instruments × average lease cost/month
    × 12)

Maintenance

    Total annual instrument maintenance cost $ _____

$$\left( \begin{array}{c} \text{Total \# leased} \\ \text{instruments} \end{array} \times \begin{array}{c} \text{total \# purchased} \\ \text{instruments} \end{array} \times \begin{array}{c} \text{average annual} \\ \text{maintenance cost} \end{array} \right)$$

Interest on Purchase Price

$$\left( \begin{array}{c} \text{Total \# instruments} \\ \text{purchased} \end{array} \times \begin{array}{c} \text{average} \\ \text{purchase} \\ \text{price} \end{array} \times \text{cost of money}/100 \right)$$

his database to show the customer's current equipment configuration. The mix includes instruments and their accessory sets and materials that are consumed by the instruments. The representative then calls up the costs that the customer incurs from the present mix. Four categories of cost contribution are shown in Figure 7-2. Taken together, the two figures give the representative a bird's-eye view of the customer's hardware and software components and their costs. The sales representative's challenge is clear: Can the customer do better?

In Figure 7-3, the representative plans a more opti-mal mix of equipment for the customer. According to the

**Figure 7-3. Equipment configuration analysis: optimal mix.**

|  | *Number per Year* | *Price* | *Annual Cost* |
|---|---|---|---|
| **Equipment** | | | |
| Instrument A-B | _____ | _____ | _____ |
| Instrument C | _____ | _____ | _____ |
| **Accessory Sets** | | | |
| Set 1-2 | _____ | _____ | _____ |
| Set 3 | _____ | _____ | _____ |
| **Materials** | | | |
| Material XX | _____ | _____ | _____ |
| Material YY | _____ | _____ | _____ |

financial analysis of this mix in Figure 7-4, the representative will learn if fewer categories of instruments and accessory sets can achieve savings for the customer over and above the costs of the present mix. If so, he will create the net benefit analysis shown in Figure 7-5, which will become the focal point of the representative's profit improvement proposal.

All customer businesses operate through mixes in their major functions. Some mixes are simply conglomerations of products. Others contain services such as training or maintenance. Others are composed of networks that are composed of systems that, in turn, are composed of subsystems. You will have to determine the mix into which you fit, what you can contribute to it in "hardware" and "software," and what dollar values of

**Figure 7-4. Financial analysis: optimal mix.**

---

Depreciation

    Total annual instrument depreciation $ _____
    (Total # instruments × average price/useful life)

Lease Cost

    Total annual instrument lease cost $ _____
    (Total # leased instruments × average lease cost/month
    × 12)

Maintenance

    Total annual instrument maintenance cost $ _____

$$\left(\begin{array}{c}\text{Total \# leased} \\ \text{instruments}\end{array} \times \begin{array}{c}\text{total \# purchased} \\ \text{instruments}\end{array} \times \begin{array}{c}\text{average annual} \\ \text{maintenance cost}\end{array}\right)$$

Interest on Purchase Price

$$\left(\begin{array}{c}\text{Total \# instruments} \\ \text{purchased}\end{array} \times \begin{array}{c}\text{average} \\ \text{purchase} \\ \text{price}\end{array} \times \text{cost of money/100}\right)$$

---

improvement you can propose. The mix becomes your market. It is the arena where you belong. Even more, it must become the arena of your expertise. You must know how to make it produce profits in the most cost-effective manner. You must know this better than anyone else in your industry. You must master the operation of the mix so well that you can present yourself to your customers as their industry's "mixmaster."

Customer mixes usually lag behind the optimal mix. They frequently represent a sizable investment. They also are tied to a customer's learning curve. Customer people have learned how to operate their current mix.

**Figure 7-5. Net benefit analysis: optimal mix.**

|  | *Optimal Mix* | *Present Mix* |
|---|---|---|
| Expenses |  |  |
| Depreciation | ———— | ———— |
| Equipment write-off | ———— | ———— |
| Lease cost | ———— | ———— |
| Maintenance | ———— | ———— |
| Interest on purchase price | ———— | ———— |
| Materials | ———— | ———— |
| Labor | ———— | ———— |
| Freight | ———— | ———— |
| Total Expense | ———— | ———— |
| Benefits |  |  |
| Investment tax credit | ———— | ———— |
| Trade-in | ———— | ———— |
| Risk management | ———— | ———— |
| Financial risk reduction (opportunity cost) | ———— | ———— |
| Instrument standardization | ———— | ———— |
| Total Benefits | ———— | ———— |
| Net expense | ———— | ———— |
| Net benefit | ———— | ———— |

They have become familiar with its capabilities and its quirks. Training programs have been built around it. Cost and production schedules are established for it. Psychologically, it has become culture, "the way we do things around here." For all these reasons, a current mix is hard to change, even with the promise of making it more optimal.

Penetration with a changed mix can only be made if there is a reason more powerful than all the reasons not to change, and if the problems of change can be made minimal. Improved productivity and profits are transcendent reasons to change. They are, to play on words, bottom-line reasons. They have more meaning than appeals to "be first," "be modern," "be competitive," or "be positioned for the future." The appeal that can win must be the appeal to "be more profitable now."

Customers know how easy it is for improved profits to be consumed by the price of change, even if change is brought about by an admittedly more optimal mix. Your key account sales teams will have to surround their financial benefits with supplementary benefit values. First, they must provide a training program to teach a customer's people how to obtain the full financial benefits of their new mix. Second, they must provide service, maintenance, and a repair, replacement, and restocking program so that the operation of the new mix can be continuous and all but minor downtime averted. Third, they must be supported by a database on the performance and profitability track record of the mix they propose. This will help them be perceived as working from a credible source, have ready answers to customer questions, and act as true students of what they sell as well as professional instructors in the field of its profit contribution.

## Making Penetration Plans Tangible

Key account penetration plans must be prepared as written documents. They should set down your positioning with each account, your penetration objectives for improved profits for both you and your customers, the penetration strategy mix that will achieve your objectives in the most cost-effective way, the profit improvement proposals that will act as deliverables for your strategies, the control procedures you will apply on each account to make certain that the improvements in profit are being delivered on time, and the essential elements of information about the customer's business required to document the plan's strategic approach.

Each penetration plan should be ratified by its customer. When it has been accepted, it should be entered into your key account database for permanent reference. Your present sales representative can have repeated access to it, as can his support teams. Other representatives can study it, incorporating strategies they find relevant to their own accounts. Newly promoted sales representatives can bring themselves quickly up-to-date on their accounts by studying the planning that has preceded them and that they must henceforth carry forward.

At the sales management level, the full roster of all penetration plans will be available for scanning. No matter how many key accounts you supervise, you will be able to call up their plans to help you manage them better, to monitor progress, to troubleshoot in advance of major problems, as well as to detect new opportunities in advance of your competitors.

Every year's plan for each customer will be an extension of its predecessors, carrying forward the progressive penetration of the account's business. Laid end-to-end, the plans will dovetail. Yet they will show significant change. Reviewing this change will be an educational experience for you and your sales representatives—and for your customers. Your ability to improve their profits will increase. Your ability to define problems to solve and to specify solutions for them will sharpen. The creativity and timeliness of your solutions will be enhanced. Your knowledge of each customer's business will expand and, with it, your business with each customer.

## Auditing Delivery of the Benefits

You should audit on at least a semiannual basis the actual penetration of each customer against plan. Your audit should focus on three areas of diagnosis:

1. Are the prime sales opportunities within each key customer's business being addressed?
2. What is your hit ratio, (the percentage of accepted proposals to those that have not been acted on in your favor)?
3. Are you neglecting any prime sales opportunities that competitors can use to gain footholds into a key customer's business?

As a result of your answers to these questions, you will know how to manage each key account team. In most cases, coaching and counseling will suffice. Remedial training may also be needed. In more extreme cases, people may have to be reallocated.

Using the penetration-planning process as your guide, you will be able to evaluate each key account sales team according to the single most important criterion controlling its performance: How much customer opportunity is the team converting into incremental profit contribution?

Figure 7-6 shows a summary form for visualizing each sales team's contribution. For each key account, it itemizes the total billed revenues that act as the gross sum from which your net incremental revenues are derived. The form tells you at a glance the net increments in the form of dollars earned and as a percentage of expenses incurred to achieve them.

The companion figures will take you behind the numbers of the key account contribution summary. Figure 7-7 shows the sales opportunities that are being realized across all key accounts. You will be able to determine how aggressively your principal solutions are being sold to benefit the major problems and opportunities of your key accounts. You will also learn how many accounts have similar problems that can be solved with the same solutions—or, if you sense an incongruity, explore why the same solution is being applied in such a broad-brush manner.

The third step in your audit is illustrated by Figure 7-8. On an individual account-by-account basis, you can analyze the profit contribution you are making to each

**Figure 7-6. Key account contribution summary.**

| Account | Total Billed Revenues ($) | Net Incremental Billed Revenues ($) | Net Incremental Billed Revenues (%) |
|---------|---------------------------|-------------------------------------|-------------------------------------|
| A | 16.5 | 2.0 | 13.1 |
| B | 16.9 | 2.2 | 14.9 |
| C | 7.5 | 0.5 | 14.6 |
| D | 9.2 | 0.7 | 15.6 |
| E | 6.2 | 0.1 | 16.7 |

**Figure 7-7. Sales opportunities across accounts.**

| Solution | Customer Problem/Opportunity | Account | | | | |
|---|---|---|---|---|---|---|
| | | A | B | C | D | E |
| | | | | | | |
| | | | | | | |
| | | | | | | |
| | | | | | | |
| | | | | | | |
| | | | | | | |
| | | | | | | |
| | | | | | | |
| | | | | | | |

**Figure 7-8. Sales opportunities within accounts.**

| Customer Division / Function | Problem / Opportunity | Solution<br>Sold (date)<br>Proposed (date)<br>To be proposed (date) | Competition (current customer standard) | Profit | |
|---|---|---|---|---|---|
| | | | | To Customer | To Us |
| | | | | | |
| | | | | | |
| | | | | | |
| | | | | | |
| | | | | | |
| | | | | | |
| | | | | | |
| | | | | | |
| | | | | | |

key customer and the profit it is contributing to you from each problem you are solving in each divisional function you have penetrated.

## Partnering the Penetration-Planning Process

As a rule, vendors plan in private against the magic moment when they will propose—a moment in which they reveal for the first time their price-performance benefits. Then, having proposed, they wait for the customer to dispose. In key account selling, the penetration plan is developed in partnership with the customer. You must take the initiative in preparing the plan. But you must invite the customer's participation in finalizing it.

The profit-improvement proposals in an account penetration plan may represent major time, dollar, and human resource investments by a customer. The improved profits you will make available can represent a call on significant incremental funds. You must acknowledge your customer's involvements. The penetration plan cannot be your plan alone. It cannot be your plan *for* a customer. To be successful, it can only be a plan made jointly *with* the customer in your mutual best interests.

Each annual plan should be an amalgam of your awareness of a customer's prime needs and the customer's own awarenesses. Before your sales teams present their proposals, they should meet with their customers' top- and bottom-tier decision makers to gain agreement on the nature and scope of the problems you have elected to solve. At the same time, they should obtain customer reaction to the profit-improvement solutions they have decided to propose. A revised target list of problems may come out of these discussions. These will be jointly determined problems, validated by the customer. Revised solutions may also emerge. These will be jointly determined solutions, endorsed at their preliminary stages by the customer. The Consultative Selling experience will be under way.

Once an annual plan is being implemented, your sales teams should review progress with their customers on a quarterly timetable. Are we focusing on the problems whose solutions are the most meaningful to you? Are there aspects of these problems that have become newly understood since our work began and that we should deal with? Is our solution being implemented according to plan? Should we anticipate snags in the next quarter? Are there migrations from our solution that we should be contemplating? Are there revisions or renovations that we should be considering? Is there an adjacent problem that we could also be solving simultaneously with the same solution?

The evaluation that coincides with the fourth quarter of a plan's implementation should be set aside for a combined review and preview meeting. What have we accomplished so far? Have we been doing what we proposed we would do? Is it working? How much incremental profits have we been able to deliver to you so far? How can we best plan the delivery of what is yet to come? Where do we go from here—what problem areas are next in line for solution? What solutions would give you the most significant results?

The review process is designed to consolidate your partnership position. You can find out where you stand based on what you have been doing. You can remind the customer of your cumulative contribution to improved profits. You can plan what comes next. By doing so, you can put yourself in position to get a head start on your forthcoming year's penetration plan and, at the same time, keep competitors out. At last but not least, you can add the new knowledge to your database on the customer's business that will enable you to improve your upcoming opportunities to sell.

# 8

# Calculating Costs-Benefits

## *How to Prove Customer Need*

When you stand before a customer in the vendor mode to sell your product, you offer its features and benefits. In turn, the customer asks you how much they cost. Because price is a cost, it is always too much. When you offer new profits in a consultative mode, customers will also ask you how much. Because you are selling money, it will never be enough.

Making more profits or contributing to them is the job of every customer manager. The top management levels plan profits strategically by determining the individual businesses in which the company will compete and what competitive advantages it will be able to bring to each of them. At every operating level below, managers contribute to achieving those overall objectives by proposing specific investment plans for top-level approval. At the top, these proposals are evaluated according to well-known specifications. Management will agree to lay out funds today in the expectation of increased future income if it meets these specifications. Given

186

these funds, your customers' managers can buy from you.

Can you add to their proposed future income? Can you add enough to be significant? Can you add it soon enough to make it valuable? Can you reduce their risk by increasing the certainty of their return on the company's investment? Is an investment with you a cost-effective way for them to make more money? If the answers are yes, you can sell new profits to your customers' middle managers on the basis of the return they yield on the customers' investments.

In order to sell this way, you must know the criteria that customers use to evaluate incremental investment opportunities so that you will be one of their preferred choices. These criteria are the specifications of projects—to be exact, the specifications of profits to be received in the future as the result of investments that must be made today.

## Contribution Margin

The key to profits is contribution margin, the amount of money each product line or business unit contributes to a customer's total profits. Affecting a customer's contribution margins is a key objective. There are two ways to do this. You can help increase sales volume at the current contribution margin. Or you can help increase contribution margin at the current volume of sales.

Figure 8-1 shows how contribution margin works. It is calculated by subtracting variable costs from sales revenues. In the example, a customer's total contribution margin is $.095. That means that each single dollar of sales is currently contributing a margin of 9.5 cents to

188                                          KEY ACCOUNT SELLING

**Figure 8-1. Analysis of profit contribution by product line ($000).**

|  | Total | Product Lines A | B | C |
|---|---|---|---|---|
| 1. Sales | $2,600 | 1,742 | 650 | 208 |
|  | % 100.0 | 67.0 | 25.0 | 8.0 |
| 2. Cost of sales | $2,106 | 1,440 | 520 | 146 |
|  | % 81.0 | 82.7 | 80.0 | 70.0 |
| 3. Gross profit (line 1 − line 2) | $ 494 | 302 | 130 | 62 |
|  | % 19.0 | 17.3 | 20.0 | 30.0 |
| 4. Wages | $ 221 | 134 | 65 | 22 |
|  | % 8.5 | 7.7 | 10.0 | 10.5 |
| 5. Other | $ 26 | 10 | 13 | 3 |
|  | % 1.0 | 0.6 | 1.9 | 1.5 |
| 6. Total (line 4 + line 5) | $ 247 | 144 | 78 | 25 |
|  | % 9.5 | 8.3 | 11.9 | 12.0 |
| 7. Contribution margin (line 3 − line 6) | $ 247 | 158 | 52 | 37 |
|  | % 9.5 | 9.0 | 8.0 | 18.0 |

cover the customer's fixed operating overhead of $221,000. It takes a lot of $1 sales to contribute enough 9.5 cents' worth of margins to cover $221,000 of overhead. Even when sales do that, the customer merely breaks even. That is where you come in. If you can increase sales or decrease the variable costs that subtract from sales revenues, you can improve customer profits.

The choices are shown in Figure 8-1. If you want to work on product line A, you can improve profits best by improving sales. While it has only a 17.3 percent gross profit, it also has a 9.0 percent contribution. Any increase in sales volume will produce new profits. On the other hand, if you work on product line B, you will have to reduce its variable costs. Its 20 percent gross profit exceeds that of A, but it is making only an 8.0 percent contribution after variable expenses. If you can reduce its expenses, you can improve its contribution even without increasing sales volume.

## Measuring Profit Improvement

Customers define a problem as a cost that *can be* reduced or a sales opportunity that *can be* realized. Customers define a solution as a cost that *has been* reduced or sales revenue that *has been* gained. In either case, customer profit has been improved.

Customers measure their solutions according to *incremental analysis*. This is sometimes called microanalysis, since it evaluates the new profit earned by a system. Three methods of incremental analysis are commonly used to measure a system's profit contribution: payback, discounted cash flow (DCF), and accounting rate of return (AROR).

### PAYBACK

The payback method measures profit improvement according to how long it will take to recoup the cash outlay required to obtain a system. Payback is essentially a criterion of "cash at risk." If payback can be achieved quickly, the risk factor will be low and the return will be high. If a system's benefits continue after payback, the return will be even higher.

### DISCOUNTED CASH FLOW

The DCF method measures profit improvement by converting the cash values of a system's costs and benefits into a present-time value. DCF analysis is usually used in conjunction with payback analysis and the AROR approach on major systems. There are two variations of the DCF method:

1. *Net present value (NPV)* applies a predetermined interest rate to discount future cash flow in order to

match it with a system's required cash outlay. The interest rate may be based on a customer's cost of capital or an arbitrary "hurdle rate" that has been set as the minimum payback for new investments. A high NPV is a customer signal to proceed.

2. *Internal rate of return (IRR)* is similar to NPV but does not contain a predetermined discount factor. The IRR is the interest rate that discounts a system's net cash flow to zero present value when compared with its required cash outlay. If the IRR rate exceeds the hurdle rate, a customer will usually proceed.

## ACCOUNTING RATE OF RETURN

The AROR method measures profit improvement by comparing the average income or expenses saved over the life of a system with the investment outlay required to obtain it. The percentage rate of return that results, based solely on the incremental income generated by the system, reflects the earnings rate of return on the incremental investment. Many customers favor this method because it is oriented to their balance sheets and income statements even though it ignores the time value of money.

All three measurement methods have certain elements in common. They all use a basic cost-benefit analysis. All of them seek to determine the present value of a system investment on a cash basis, including the opportunity costs involved; the operating revenue; the operating costs; and the difference between operating revenue and operating costs, which equals the benefits.

Of the three methods, only AROR relates to the return on investment (ROI), which is used to evaluate total customer company performance. This total ROI must be narrowed down to AROR in order to evaluate an *incremental investment,* such as a specific system. A system's AROR can, therefore, be considered as the added rate of profit that the system can add to the customer's ROI.

### AROR/ROI INTERRELATIONSHIPS

The interrelationship between ROI and AROR can be seen by the similarity between their formulas:

$$\text{ROI} = \frac{\text{net profit}}{\text{sales}} \times \frac{\text{sales}}{\text{investment}}$$

$$\text{AROR} = \frac{\text{net profit}}{\text{investment}}$$

For calculating AROR, sales are eliminated from the ROI formula because total customer company analysis is not relevant for most systems investments. The impact of most systems, even huge, capital-intensive systems, becomes swallowed up in a customer's total ROI. The consultant cannot identify an individual system's contribution when it is dispersed over such a broad base. Therefore, to make a system's incremental contribution measurable, its impact should be calculated according to AROR.

Net income is not the sole basis for determining AROR. Gross profit may be an appropriate measure of a system's income if no incremental operating costs are involved or if operating costs cannot be separated on incremental sales. Contribution margin may also be an appropriate measure of system income if no incremental fixed costs are incurred or if fixed costs cannot be separated.

## The ROI Yardstick

To tell whether the increased sales you propose from a profit-improvement project are good or poor, you will need an accurate yardstick. In many selling organizations, profit is commonly expressed as a percentage of sales price or as an absolute amount per unit. But any method of measuring profit as percentage of sales is insufficient for consultative purposes since it takes into account only two elements of profit: sales revenues and cost. The difference between them is then calculated as a percentage of sales. Most companies call that difference profit. Profit, however, has a very important third component: time.

From the point of view of return, profit can be regarded as the ratio of income earned during an operating cycle to the amount of capital invested to produce it. Thus profits have two costs: time costs and costs of producing the product or service. When profit is compared with its funded investment, it is being expressed as an ROI.

ROI is an analytic tool that, for sales purposes, has three qualities in its favor:

1. It is a fair measurement of profit contribution.
2. It is helpful in directing attention to the most immediate profit opportunities, allowing them to be ranked on a priority basis.
3. It is likely to be readily understood and accepted by business function managers and sales and marketing managers of your customer companies.

Figure 8-2 represents the formulas for calculating ROI. The formulas relate the major operating and finan-

## Figure 8-2. ROI formulas.

A. Options for improving ROI by improving turnover

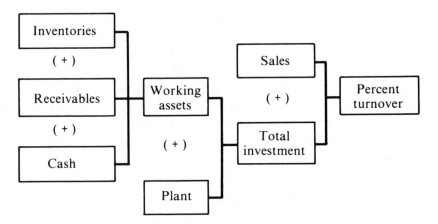

B. Options for improving ROI by improving operating profit

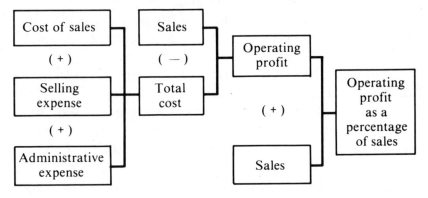

cial factors required in profit making to the rate used to measure the profit that is made: the rate of profit per unit sales in dollars, the rate of turnover of operating funds, the funds required to finance business operations, and the total investment of capital employed, including working assets, plants, and facilities.

The customer's sole economic justification for investing in your profit-improvement projects is to earn a superior rate of return on the funds invested. This truism must be interpreted in two ways. One is terms of income gained. The other is in terms of costs avoided in obtaining investment funds, costs of retaining such funds, and costs suffered by denying their use for alternative, potentially more profitable projects.

Diagnosis lies at the heart of sales consulting. Assessment techniques that are based on return on investment lie at the heart of diagnosis.

As Figure 8-2 shows, ROI is the product of the rate of operating profit, expressed as a percentage of sales, and the rate of turnover. Anytime you want to improve a customer's ROI, you must first diagnose a problem in operating rate or an opportunity in turnover.

Part A of Figure 8-2 shows the ingredients of ROI expressed as turnover. If you examine each of those ingredients, you will find profit opportunities that can improve turnover. You can, for example, recommend a project to reduce the amount of funds invested in working assets, thus reducing the customer's total investment base. As a result, you can improve your customer's profit without increasing sales volume.

Part B shows options for diagnosing profit improvement if your objective is to increase operating profit. You can recommend a project to lower the customer's cost of sales. This will reduce total costs and enable the customer to show an increase in operating profit.

## Opportunity Identification

The ROI approach is the best diagnostic tool to identify opportunities. As the ROI formula shows, opportunity is always present when either a customer's operating profit rate or turnover can be improved.

Any system must meet customer standards of what constitutes an adequate return on investment. A system whose promise of profit improvement falls below this standard will probably be rejected as not being worth the investment. It will usually be ruled out by one of three standards for determining whether a given rate of return on investment is adequate: its investment exceeds the basic cost of money, its payback is too risky, or the return falls below the amount that customers believe they have the right to expect.

Customers who invest money to acquire your products or services obtain an asset. Their job is to turn it over as quickly as possible so that it will revert to cash. Then they can reinvest in another asset with you and start the process over again. If they make good investments with you, they will end each investment cycle with more money than they started with. Asset turnover is the secret to making money. The more assets that are turned, and the faster they are turned over, the more money will be made. It is therefore in your own best interest to help.

Accounts receivable and inventory are a customer's two major "current assets." You can convert current assets to cash by turning them over. Anything you can do to speed up a customer's asset turnover in these two areas will make money for both of you. If you and a customer allow these assets to build up—if a customer's sales decline and inventories grow or if your customer's customers delay paying their bills—both of you will be in trouble.

Ideally, customers would like to have zero investments in accounts receivable and inventory. Every day that you can help them condense their collection period is money in the bank. Every additional turn of inventory also improves profits. An item that turns over 1.7 times a year sits in inventory approximately seven months before being sold. If you can help move it in six months, you can accelerate its contribution to earnings by one-seventh.

Asset turnover is especially important in selling to a key customer's profit center managers. They are evaluated on the basis of ROIs. Their ROI is calculated by dividing their earnings by the investment in their asset base. The higher their ROI, the greater the investment that top management will continue to make in their profit centers and the higher the reward each center's manager will receive.

The ROI of your customers is a good index of how good a partner you are. If you have the ability to affect inventory but you let their money remain tied up in inventories that do not turn, you are a poor partner. If you have the ability to affect collections but you let their money remain tied up in accounts receivable, you are a poor partner. Increasing inventory turns and decreasing collection cycles will make you better.

## Calculating Investment Risk

Whenever you make a proposal to a customer manager, you are challenging him to calculate a risk. If you ask him to invest with you to expand his capacity to produce one of his existing products, you are offering him a median risk. All other types of investment will have a higher or lower risk. Investments for replacement or repair are the safest. Past experience can accurately help foretell their probable cash flows. Cost-reduction investments are somewhat riskier. No one can calculate the exact magnitude of their potential savings. The riskiest type of investment concerns new products or new market development where neither the costs nor the revenues can be predicted with certainty.

As soon as a customer manager invests with you, he incurs an opportunity cost equal to the return he could have earned from an alternative investment of the same funds. The opportunity cost is in addition to the direct cost he pays you and the indirect costs he incurs in implementation. The further away you take him from his median risk where he knows the return he can expect, the more risk-averse he will be, the more proof he will demand, and the closer partnership with you he will expect.

Whenever risk increases, a customer manager will balance it against its return. In high-risk situations, the customer manager will be more interested in whether the return is sufficient to justify the risk than the rate of return itself, however high it may be.

The risk-return trade-off is the basis of management. The only fully known sum of money in any transaction is its investment. Future benefits are always uncertain. As risk increases, the anticipated return must increase with it. If a manager is confronted with two equal investments that promise a similar return, he will probably choose the investment with the lower risk—that is, the one with the highest net present value (NPV) per dollar invested.

Where risk is equal or minimal, it is not a factor. Under these conditions, making an investment is preferable to letting money sit idle—and thereby incurring opportunity cost—as long as a positive NPV can be returned. This means that the value received by a customer must equal or exceed his cost of capital. As long as it does either one or the other, the investment will be acceptable. This is simply another way of calculating the worth of an investment based on its NPV. According to NPV, investing $50 million today for a stream of future cash flows with a value today of $59.755 million is an acceptable investment. In effect, the customer is paying $50 million for an asset worth $59.755 million, gaining $9.755 million of new value. Since the NPV is well over zero, this is a good investment. If it were only zero, the customer manager's wealth would be unchanged and his time wasted.

Risk, no matter how calculable, increases over time. That is one reason why a dollar today is always worth more than a dollar in the future. Two other reasons why money has a time value are inflation and the opportunity cost that is incurred when money is not being productively invested. The price of delay in receiving money equals the cost of the return on the best investment that could have been made for it.

Because money has a time value, every dollar returned by an investment is worth less as time goes on. For example, two dollars invested for a 10 percent annual return a year later is worth ninety-one cents today. A year from now it will be worth eighty-three cents. This is how your customer manager thinks about investments. He says that if he has ninety-one cents on hand today, he can invest it with this supplier at 10 percent interest and it will grow into one dollar within one year. "Is this the best deal available to me at this time?" he asks. "Can I get a better rate of interest anywhere else? Can I get a quicker payback? Can I get a larger return?"

# 9

# Gaining Competitive Advantage

## *How to Propose Added Customer Values*

The way you are prepared to serve key accounts becomes your market position. You get the type of customers you are positioned for. They become your natural partners. They are attracted to you because of their situation: Their phase of the life cycle focuses their attention to costs and you are positioned as cost reducers, or their life-cycle phase forces their attention to sales and you are positioned as sales developers.

If you are positioned as a *cost reducer,* you will attract two kinds of customers:

1. Start-up businesses that want to avoid unnecessary sunk costs.
2. Mature businesses that want to eliminate some of their cost centers or cut back on their downscaling impact on profits.

If you are positioned as a *sales developer,* you will attract two kinds of customers:

1. Entry businesses that want to make it fast to break-even.
2. Growth businesses that want to keep growing fast.

If you can improve customer profits by both cost reduction and sales development, you can be a full partner. Otherwise, you can only be a half partner. Whichever half you choose presents a paradox. It is easier to prove profit improvement by cost reduction because direct costs are hard numbers. Sales opportunities, on the other hand, represent opportunity losses. Their numbers are softer and more subject to assumption. But no customer can save his way to prosperity. Sooner or later, he must increase earnings from sales if he is going to grow. So sales development, which is more difficult than cost reduction to quantify as well as to achieve, is more necessary if you are going to play a commanding role in improving the profits of key accounts.

If you can develop significant new sales for your customers, they can tolerate unnecessary costs. But if you can only reduce costs, they cannot long tolerate the lack of new sales without falling into the most stagnant mode of business, stability.

A stable business is going nowhere, neither growing nor declining. It is indecisive, inactive, and indolent. Decisions take forever. There is hope that the need for them will go away while they are being deliberated. The stable business lives in fear. Its managers are afraid to attempt to grow the business because, if they fail, the added investment without return will plunge the business into decline. As a result, managers of stable businesses characteristically look down, not up, awaiting the fall and suspecting that every action—indeed, any action—

will unbalance their tentative harmony of earnings and expenses.

Stable businesses make the worst partners. They are candidates for cost reduction but only if the costs to be reduced significantly exceed the costs incurred to reduce them and if results show up quickly. To help make sure that this is always the case, stable business managers invest as little as possible against the chance, however slight, that the funds may prove unrecoverable. Even if their investments are productive, their returns on this basis are likely to be equally small. The consequent net improvement is apt to be miniscule.

A stable business is a paradox to its own management and to any supplier business that would attempt to grow it. Businesses in stability may be grown but they do not dare to grow. They have lost their dynamic. Only when they start to decline can they be partnerable. In the decline phase of maturity there is no choice. Sales must be developed. But more important, costs must be reduced in a major way. The fear of falling, which induces paralysis during stability, is gone. The fear of going belly-up, which induces action, replaces it.

## Selling to the Customer's Position

Given the choice, sales will almost always be awarded to the specialist over the generalist supplier of products, services, systems or "solutions." The specialist knows the customer's industry. He knows the customer's business. He knows the customer's process whose profit contribution must be improved by his solution, and he knows the customer's dependence on the process at the specific position in the customer life cycle that the specialist affects: What the customer's business objectives are at his point in the cycle and how he can meet them more fully, more quickly, and more surely by making an impact on the contribution of the process.

## POSITIONING TO SELL TO CUSTOMERS IN START-UP

Some start-ups are the key customers of the future. They represent major risk, both to you and to themselves. Start-up is the single most crucial phase of the customer life cycle. Entry and growth, the two following phases, are preconditioned by start-up. A good start will not necessarily predict the good growth that characterizes a key account. But a poor start will largely foredoom it.

Two events take place at start-up that forecast the coming attractiveness of a business. One is that a market database is laid down. The other is that the product's value-to-price relationship is determined. These events set the *who,* the *what,* and the *how much* for the business. If you are able to partner at the start-up phase, getting in on the ground floor, you can help influence each of these critical factors. Not only can you become invaluable; you can build yourself into the continuing evolution of the customer's business as one of its vital components while it moves through the successive stages of its commercial life.

Let us take a new start-up venture within a mature corporation. Without knowing anything more, just that it is a start-up, you know what the manager's objective must be. He must move quickly through his start-up cycle, move "out of the garage" and into his market as soon as possible. He is on a borrowed budget and on borrowed time. His management will wait only so long for him to produce results. His competitors are not waiting at all. Meanwhile, for every day that passes, his market opportunity window may be closing.

What approach should you take? You must address the business's life position. Since you know that market entry is a start-up manager's fixation, your dialogue should focus on it. Can you help the manager make entry on time? Even better, earlier? Less expensively? Can you help him stay there once he gets there by ensuring his product's reliability and avoiding recall? Can you help him make sure he is choosing the right market and has positioned himself properly in its perceptions?

Your answers will be the basis for your sales to start-ups.

## PROPOSING TO A START-UP

A start-up proposal must be primarily based on cost avoidance in preparing for market entry. Secondarily, it can be based on preventing loss of sales opportunity.

Before it makes market entry, a new business is a collection of sunk costs. While its asset base is being planned and laid down, nothing is available for sale. Hence, its cash flow is negative. The capital funds that have been appropriated for it are being invested at a high rate of expenditure. Everything is going out. Nothing is coming in.

How many of these costs can be avoided? Every dollar saved at this point is a dollar-plus earned later. A dollar that can be saved can immediately be invested elsewhere. Or it can be returned to the start-up's sponsor. This lowers its total investment and, by reducing its eventual break-even point, speeds payback.

Start-ups are heavily into cost displacement or cost replacement. Your proposals should therefore wipe out a cost category or consolidate several costs into a single lower cost. They should substitute a less costly solution like automation for a more costly investment like human labor. The sum total of what they save can be regarded as the equivalent of profits from sales that cannot yet be made.

The second area of start-up proposing is reducing the threat of incurring opportunity costs that can delay market entry or can come back to haunt a business after it has been commercialized. These opportunity areas typically involve four business functions: market analysis to make sure the market is rightly assessed from the start; product and process design to make sure that the product is right and is manufactured cost-effectively; quality assurance to make sure that the product will not incur excessive warranty costs for repair or costs for replacement or recall; and forecasting and inventory control to make sure that the product is neither back-ordered, causing lost sales; nor overstocked, causing excessive handling, storage, and insurance costs.

## POSITIONING TO SELL TO CUSTOMERS IN ENTRY

Entry is the make-or-break event for a business. It furnishes the proof of start-up. The test of start-up is how little needs to be done at entry—or redone—to refine and redefine the actions taken in start-up. A good start-up leaves little to be done at entry except power up for volume operations. The rescaling of output places tremendous pressure on a business. It threatens quality control and all the functions that are dedicated to manufacturing and marketing. Schedules must be met, downtime and recall avoided, and early warnings heeded.

Entry allows the first checkpoint at which market segmentation can be evaluated. Was the right market selected? Entry also validates the value-to-price ratio.

Will the market pay full margins for the value? The growth phase yet to come depends on the accuracy of these start-up decisions. If they are shown to be wrong at entry, growth will be delayed or denied. The business may have to go back to the drawing board—that is, back to start-up—for rework.

Helping a start-up business make its entry on time and on plan, and then making it through entry as quickly as possible to begin growth, is the greatest contribution you can make to a customer. Only by reaching break-even does a business become a new commercial entity. Up to then, it is merely an investment, an act of faith that there is an opportunity for a profitable return. The advent of break-even is the signal that faith has paid off. At this point, no one knows how much the payoff will be. But at least there will be one, and until this point is reached there can be no chance at all to make a big winner happen.

Let us take a customer business that is just entering its market: a successful start-up. Without knowing anything more, just that it is an entrant, you know what the manager's objective must be. He must consolidate his precarious initial toehold into a firm foothold by reaching break-even and bringing in promised profits. Every unnecessary day below break-even adds to his costs, postpones his profits, and increases his vulnerability. His management's patience may run out, or a competitor may become profitable first and plow back the first profits into accelerated sales and advertising. The market's money may go elsewhere.

What approach should you take? You must address the business's life position. Since you know that break-even and the onset of positive cash flow are an entrant manager's fixations, your dialogue should focus on them. Can you help the manager enter faster? Less expensively? Can you help him maintain his product within specifications and in stock? Can you help him bill and collect receivables faster to guarantee cash flow? Can you help him remain differentiated from the inevitable knock-off competitors who will be attracted by his success and unencumbered by his costs?

Your answers will be the basis for your sales to entrants.

## PROPOSING TO AN ENTRY

An entry proposal must be primarily based on sales generation and secondarily on preventing the opportunity loss of even further sales.

Immediately on its market entry, a business presses for break-even. This is the milestone that signals the payback of its founding investment. To achieve continuing growth, it must focus on maximizing revenues and earnings from sales.

How many more incremental sales dollars can be brought in? How much faster can they be booked? How much faster can they be collected and converted into receipts? Or, to say the same things in other words, how fast can the market be penetrated, how fully and completely can its opportunity be capitalized, and how great a percentage of sales can be realized?

Every qualified prospect who remains unsold represents an opportunity cost. Every customer who buys one unit but could have bought two represents opportunity cost.

Entry proposals must pay equal attention to internal factors that can influence the outflow of product and the inflow of revenue. Forecasting and inventory must be attuned to the market's drive. Quality must be maintained. Downtime must be minimized lest it cut off the flow of marketable products. These business functions must be treated as sales aids, supporting an entry business management's preoccupation with moneymaking and not dealing with them as contributors to cost. At entry, as in growth, direct costs are comparatively irrelevant.

## POSITIONING TO SELL TO CUSTOMERS IN GROWTH

The reward for withstanding the enormous pressure of passing quickly through entry is the privilege of accepting the prolonged pressure of growth. The growth phase of a business is its finest hour. Everything that has been planned for so long now can come together in the race for volume—for production, for productivity, and for market share. Time is of the essence. Demand, once provoked, must be fulfilled. Competition, once enticed, must be preempted.

Two other events mark growth. The product quality set at entry must be standardized so that reliability becomes the product's middle name. Reliability—no surprises—is the keystone to growth. Its assurance must be warranted. At the same time that the product is being standardized for volume output, the demand that has been created for it in the marketplace must be fully met. Every unmet unit of demand represents opportunity loss. To make certain that demand is fully capitalized, growth is the phase to begin the start-up of a product family. What will the next product be? How will it complement, supplement, or implement the product being grown?

If you position yourself to sell growth businesses, you must address three areas of customer need: You must help maximize volume, help enforce standardization, and help generate the follow-on products that will add up to a growth family. In these three ways, the customer's original growth curve can be driven as high as possible and held high for as long as possible. This is the common interest of both of you. Simultaneously, while the customer's positive cash flow is high, new investments can be made in a successor growth curve that, at first, will reinforce its predecessor and later may replace its contribution.

Let us take a customer business that is growing: a successful entrant. Without knowing anything more, just that it is growing, you know what the manager's objective must be. He must continue to grow at an increasing rate. If his rate of growth slows, maturity may overtake the business and the opportunity to become a big winner will be foreclosed. If the market for the business is growing and the customer is only growing along at par with it, then each dollar of unmade sales growth represents opportunity loss that can never be made up.

What approach should you take? You must address the business's life position. Since you know that the business growth rate is a growth manager's fixation, your dialogue should focus on it. Can you help the manager ensure productivity, minimize downtime, and assure consistency by manufacturing a standard product with zero defects? Can you help increase sales to the original market or extend them into adjacent markets? Can you help control variable costs that invariably inflate with volume? Can you help prepare for the first product proliferation that will extend the initial line into a product family?

Your answers will be the basis for your sales to growth businesses.

## PROPOSING TO A GROWTH BUSINESS

A growth proposal must be primarily based on accelerating the customer's sales that begin with entry. It must also be concerned with preventing the opportunity cost of lost sales.

A customer's growth phase has two objectives. The first is to maximize market entry by selling up to the full manufacturing capacity of the business. This puts the emphasis on gaining market share as quickly as possible and driving the growth curve as high as it can go. A growth business has an insatiable appetite. It devours cash. Therefore, cash flow must be ensured. It is a cardinal sin to lose sales because lack of cash or capacity prevents their fulfillment. This means that productivity must be maintained, with its quality tightly controlled. Nothing suffocates growth like the inability to get product out the door except the inability to keep it from coming back.

How much faster can the customer's business be grown? How much faster can inventory be turned and receivables collected? How can downtime be minimized and quality maintained?

A customer's second objective in the growth phase is to prepare the business for its next entry. A successful market entry not only justifies proliferation; it demands it. Market acceptance offers opportunity for market expansion.

How cost-effectively can a second entry follow? What economies can be gained by sharing asset bases? How can the initial product's reputation for quality be bred into the next product? How can tie-in sales create a system for selling the first and second products together?

The transcendent purpose of growth is to perpetrate growth. How long can a growth rate of sales and profit making be maintained? Since growth is a rate and not a state, this is the key question. Every additional day that the rate of growth can be sustained is an added day of premium profits—one day more during which the onset of the declining margins of maturity can be postponed.

## POSITIONING TO SELL TO CUSTOMERS IN MATURITY

A customer in maturity has an upside and a downside. The upside is that, by the time a business has become mature, its managers believe that they know just about everything that has to do with how it should be run. This is also its downside. When everything is perceived to be known, innovation is difficult. Lack of innovation is the precise reason why a business becomes mature in the first place.

At maturity, the volume dependency that had been built up in growth has become chronic. The learning curve that brings down unit costs along with volume is, at the same time, a stern taskmaster. As volume becomes relentless, the pressure mounts to increase the share of market necessary to absorb it. This can usually be accomplished only by accepting progressively lower margins. As a result, the watch on costs becomes a customer's main preoccupation.

If you position yourself to sell to mature customers, you will have four major areas of opportunity. Your major duty is to keep mature customers mature—that is, to keep them in business as profitable entities whose return meets their corporate hurdle rate for sustained investment. Your next duty is to keep mature customers in business in the United States. Otherwise, you may find that you have grown the customers but lost the business.

The art of keeping a mature customer profitable requires a fine balance between reducing costs and cost-effectively increasing sales. Cost reductions will keep a customer in the ballgame, making up for margin shrinkage. But only by adding to market share can a customer grow. Share must be sold, not bought, if it is to be a genuine contributor to renewed earnings. Since mature market size is stable at best, or more likely to be on the way down, each slice of incremental market share must come out of a competitor's share. This makes share building expensive and frequently only transient, up for grabs by any competitor willing to risk cost control to seize share.

Mature customers are collections of cost centers. Even though customers acquire considerable skills in controlling them, if you can reduce them even further you will always have a job. Since the cumulative costs at maturity are usually large, only a small percentage reduction is required for you to be welcome.

The same is true for a mature customer's share of market. The larger the share, the greater the value of only a small increment. In markets where the dollar value of each share point is worth several millions, gains of small fractions of a single percentage point can make a considerable impact on profits. The key, of course, is that gains must not cost more than they are worth.

You must ask two questions of a mature customer. The first is "How can we grow you?" The answers will be in terms of reduced costs and increased sales. The second question poses a greater challenge: "How can we grow a renewed life cycle for you in your existing business?"

The first question will steer you toward decreasing operating expenses, stimulating technology, and invigorating a customer's marketing functions. The second question makes an entirely different set of demands. It invites you to partner with the customer to make his business recompetitive.

What new technological opportunities can be exploited? What market opportunities? What forms of strategic alliances can be most cost-efficient: joint ventures, R&D partnerships, or marketing partnerships? With a successful outcome, you can not only create growth; you can create a new growable customer with whom you are naturally partnered from the inception.

Let us take a customer business that has become mature. Without knowing anything more, just that it is mature, you know what the manager's objective must be. He must ensure the competitiveness of his business by reducing its costs and increasing its productivity so that it can be among its industry's low-cost, high-efficiency producers. In a mature industry where commodity products have lost their differentiation and where the size of the market may not be expandable, low cost and increased cost-effectiveness are the only available strategies for margin protection.

What approach should you take? You must address the business's life position. Since you know that cost control and productivity improvement are a mature manager's fixations, your dialogue should focus on them. Can you help the manager reduce his labor content? Can you help reduce scrap and downtime? Can you help increase volume without increasing costs? Can you decrease costs? Can you add product value through marginal renovation? Can you increase market share at competitive expense?

Your answers will be the basis for your sales to mature businesses.

## PROPOSING TO A MATURE BUSINESS

Proposal to a mature business must be primarily based on delaying the decline of profit per sale that is the inevitable result of the end point of growth. Even though volume at maturity may be huge, decaying margins and increasing costs absorb revenues at an increasing rate as maturity progresses. The mature phase of a business therefore requires a delicate balance between maintaining or increasing sales yet maintaining or decreasing costs, including the cost of sales. The expansion of sales is more difficult in mature markets where the markets themselves are not growing and increased penetration requires the conquest of a portion of a competitor's share. How can sales be maintained more economically? How can the product be renovated marginally to provide a sales incentive yet keep costs down? How can costs— any costs, all costs—be better controlled?

Mature proposals must focus heavily on productivity improvement as a means of increasing output at lower or the same cost. By the time a business becomes mature, its asset base has become a mixed blessing. It provides the capability base of the business. But it also provides its cost base. Can it be reduced? Can it be modernized? Can it be made more productive? Buying instead of making, leasing instead of buying, operating jointly instead of going it alone can provide alternatives to cost.

Just as growth proposals are dedicated to perpetuating the growth phase, mature proposals must perpetuate maturity as long as possible. How long can the business go on yielding an acceptable rate of return on its assets before the assets become more valuable than their return? This is the key question for mature proposing. Every additional day that the return from a mature business can be sustained at an acceptable rate is an added day of cash flow and market presence—one day more during which divestiture can be postponed.

# 10

# Implications and Applications

---

What are the implications of key account selling? What can you expect when you apply it to your business?

When a supplier decides to concentrate on its key accounts, it changes more than the way it manages its principal sales strategy. It alters the nature of the sales function itself. It revises forever the relationship it shares with its major customers. And it provides a platform for taking unusually innovative approaches to the ways it goes about earning its growth profits.

## Bringing the Customer in

The strategy of key account selling may suggest a one-way objective, penetrating customer businesses at high decision levels. In reality, penetration works both ways. While you are broadening and deepening your presence inside customer businesses, the customer knowledge that is being gained is flowing back into your own operations. The customer is being brought in.

Nothing more salubrious can happen to the sales function. The customer has always been its missing link. Historically, it has contained product knowledge, process knowledge, pricing knowledge, and promotional knowledge in profusion. These are all internal areas of information that have dramatized the "me-ness" of most sales functions. Rarely have they been sufficiently customer-oriented to the "they" out there. The closest to knowing about what goes on "out there" has been competitive knowledge. But even this has been more or less focused on competitive products, processes, pricing, and promotion.

Key account selling internalizes your customers. It brings them inside your business in the form of data about their most significant problems and opportunities that you can affect. The data do more than simply represent each customer; they define your opportunities in terms of the customer's problems that you can help solve and the customer's opportunities that you can help achieve.

These two shorthand ways of describing a customer are the same attributes by which your customers think of themselves. "We are these unsolved problems, and here are their costs to us. We are these unachieved opportunities, and here are their values to us. When we quantify our costs and our values, we arrive at our objectives. This is what we are really all about."

Bringing customers into your business means knowing their cost problems, and the values they assign to their opportunities, and knowing their objectives. Their objectives are their targets. They will try to reach them by two types of strategies. One will aim to solve their cost problems. The other will seek to expand their sales opportunities. Key account selling allows you to help them do both. But you can only help them if you know what they know.

To bring your customers into your business means never having to say you don't know.

When customers are inside your decision-making system, you will not be able to ignore them at the all-important initial stages of proposal, where all sales are really made. The presence of customer knowledge in your database will affect not only your decisions but how you go about making them. "Get the customer in here"—in the form of customer data—will become your most insistent demand. Without these data, you will be embarrassed at your cerebral nakedness.

Customers, no longer strangers, outsiders, or adversaries, will become familiar. You will get the feel of their businesses. Their problems and opportunities will be your starting points for selling—not your products, how they are made, or how they perform and what their price may be. All of these vendor sales points will become subservient to what you know about your customers. If they have value, it will be in relation to adding operating and financial value to your customers. If there is no value they can add, there is no value they can claim.

## Diffusing Traditional Buyer-Seller Roles

When customers have been brought into your business as residents in your sales database, and when you have penetrated their businesses in depth, breadth, and height, the traditional distinctions between buyer and seller will become diffused. Their basis, which lies in the absence of mutual objectives, will have disappeared. Win-lose sales strategies will have no place. Because your customers must win if you are going to have a growing market, and because you must win if your customers are going to have you as a growing improver of their profit, your combined need for win-win relations will foster a new mutuality in your roles.

The line between selling and buying will gray out. The zones where customer interests conflict with your interests will thin down. Your need to overcome your customers—to sell them aggressively by defeating their resistance—will be converted to a need on your part to come over to their way of assigning priorities to their problems, defining the kinds of solutions they can most readily accept, and together with them, implementing the solutions inside their businesses.

You will still have to compete to serve them. But once accepted, you will become collaborators, the kind who are called partners in profit. Your common objectives will be identified in your account penetration plans. Both of you will have signed off on them. The plans' strategies will also be known to both of you, approved by your customers so that they and their people can work together with you and your people to achieve your shared objectives.

In such a scenario, which is already commonplace in many key account relationships, who is buyer and who is seller—and what difference does it make? Your role will be that of a customer extender, acting as an extension of your customer's own people and their capabilities to solve the customer's problems. As an extension of customer capabilities, you can become positioned as a true adder of value. Your contribution is perceptible. It is also quantifiable.

The essence of role blending is the combined ability of you and your customer to achieve the dollar objectives of your account penetration plan. This is your pivot

point in moving away from vending. If you fail, you fall
back to being a vendor. You separate out of the blend
and become a supplier once again, perceived as having
your own self-serving objectives that are bound to be
inconsistent with the needs of your customer.

Vendors are readily identifiable as vendors, and
vending is a well-accepted role. If you want to depart
from it to take on more of a partnered positioning, the
burden of proof will be on you. You must signal your
new position in unmistakable terms by demonstrating
that you deserve to be permitted access to top-tier
managers. You must also earn access to top-tier information about the customers' business problems and
opportunities. These are privileges not accorded to vendors. If you want to qualify for them, you must qualify
for a partnership with your customers in the pursuit of
their supreme objective—profit.

## Taking a Financial Service Position

The one-to-one linkage of being positioned as a partner
in the achievement of your customers' objectives tells
you exactly what your sales posture must be: You will
have to sell a financial benefit. This will require you to
take on aspects of a service business whose product is
money, expressed in one form or another, and whose
basic process is the appreciation of customer net worth.
When customers have completed each of their transactions with you, they should possess a greater value than
they had at the onset, even after paying your price. This
is the nature of a financial service.

To the extent that the improved value of their operations is significant and consistent, your customers will

know whether you are a good partner with whom to do business or only an imperfectly disguised vendor.

Selling a financial benefit imposes a number of specific demands on how you train, reward, and manage a key account sales force. You will have to teach them to know enough about the effect of their products, equipment, or systems on a customer's business to be able to calculate the degree of improved value they can contribute. You will also have to teach them the language in which financial values are expressed and the fundamental arithmetic that is involved in arriving at a determination of costs, profits, break-even points, present values, and returns on investments.

Sales representatives who sell money values and whose personal expertise is instrumental in deriving those values—both for their customers and for their own company—ought to be compensated in some proportion to the profits they improve. They can be paid a bonus on the amount of incremental profits they deliver to their accounts, for example. This will help ensure the commonality of their objectives with customer objectives. To make sure that they respect the dual requirements of their mission, their bonus on customer profits can be conditioned by minimum profit returns that you expect them to earn for your own business. A kicker can be added to the bonus in cases where their achievement exceeds preset boundaries.

The act of managing a financial service sales force is principally an exercise in total commitment. You must guard against defining your product as solely what you make instead of the values from it that you sell. You must also guard against ceaseless pressures from your customers that test your commitment to consult with them rather than to vend. They will try to determine how serious you are, so they can get comfortable with their own commitment to consult with you. In addition, they will always be probing the capabilities of your sales force to bring them improved values.

A financial service sales force, more than any other, lives or dies on its ability to create measurable and attributable gains on a customer's bottom line. The gains must be guaranteed in dollar terms. The customer must be able to attribute them to you. You must be able to do it again. The customer's added profit between "before" and "after" is your "product." There is no way to hide it if it is significant. Nor is there a way to hide from it if it is not. Your emphasis on performance must therefore be unrelenting. You and your key account representatives perform in the most visible corporate fishbowl of all when you elect to sell profit. It is not that you must be more accountable than if you manage a vendor sales force. You must, though, be much more responsible to your key customers. For a vendor, a one-time failure in product performance is survivable. Profit that has been promised by a partner but does not materialize may not be.

## Optimizing Key Account Contribution

The fact that a customer is a key account does not mean that all your transactions will automatically be the big-winner type that yield both of you major amounts of profits. The 80-20 rule mandates that as many as 80 percent of all transactions produce only as little as 20 percent of any key account sales team's profit contribution. It is the remaining 20 percent of your transactions that makes a key account relationship productive of growth profits.

The single most critical standard of performance for

managing a key account sales force is to provide a systematic method for concentrating the time and talent of your representatives on the most productive proposals.

What composes the 80 percent and what composes the 20 percent?

The bulk of key account transactions generally consist of proposing more or less repetitive solutions to standard, recurrent problems: improving profit by advancing the collection of receivables or by decreasing inventory carrying costs or by increasing productivity of a business function or by stepping up turnover. These problems may prevail throughout a key account's operating divisions. Or they may be epidemic only in a single division's business units. Sometimes every account in the same industry will have identical problems, because they come with the industry. To deal with them most cost-effectively, you should develop virtually standardized solutions that can be proposed, installed, and monitored in a virtually standardized manner.

Standardized solutions to standard, recurrent problems will release selling time and talent for allocation to the second category of key account sales.

Two types of situations compose this 20 percent category. One is made up of semistandardized solutions to standard problems that feature a difference from the first category: They have a one-time uniqueness about them that makes a standardized solution unworkable. The second type of situation is the custom-tailored solution. This represents the apex of your ability to apply your expertise to solve what is usually an exceptional— or once-in-a-long-time—problem of major importance to a customer's business. The custom-tailored solution must be your highest-ticket item, because it reflects the highest value that you can confer on a customer.

Custom-tailored solutions can provide multiple profit opportunities. Initially, they yield premium profits based on their premium value for the original customer. Next, they can generate additional premium profits by adaptation to closely similar problems, either with the same customer or with others in the same industry. Eventually, some of them can become semistandardized or standardized solutions for sale to several key accounts.

The more you can focus on selling customized solutions, the greater opportunity you will have to maximize the contribution you can make to your key customers as well as the contribution you receive from them. This is the classic challenge of managing a key account sales force.

## Summing Up the Key Account Mission

Bringing the customer into your key account planning will radicalize your sales performance. Once the customer is in, you can justly describe your operations as customer-driven and market-oriented. Once in, your sales force can begin to build customer acceptance from the very start of their proposal process instead of only hoping to obtain it at the end. Once in, the connection between your customer's profits and your own will become bonded. Neither of you will ever let the other forget it.

If you accept these implications of managing a key account sales force, you will be able to take command of sales management's fundamental task: maximizing the value of your most perishable resource, the time that is available to your key account representatives to spend with their top-tier decision makers. This is "time on target,'' the most critical and elusive element in selling. Because it is dispensed at the pleasure of your key account customers, it cannot be bought, cajoled, or consistently manipulated. It can only be earned.

The entry and reentry price for penetrating the top tier is the same. Your representatives must bring new learning about customer profit improvement. This is the output of their database. They must also bring new achievement. This is the output of their proposals. These two components of the partnering process—new learning about customer problems and new achievements in solving them—are the end products of key account selling.

''For the first time,'' your key account representatives will say, ''I feel that my customers are really listening to me. And why not? It's their businesses I'm talking about, not mine. They want me to sell, because they want the improved profits they know I can bring. As a result, it's no longer clear to me whose job I'm doing, theirs or mine. It's no longer clear to them, either. Maybe that's why we're working so well together.''

# Appendix 1

## *Superproduct Strategy for Key Account Sales to High-Growth Industries*

Fast-growing industries do not necessarily have more needs than industries whose growth is slower or took place some time ago. They do, though, have more urgent needs. They require immediate benefits in order to continue their rate of growth. Their downside risk is that growth will slow, never to regain its thrust unless problems are solved and opportunities are seized at once. For this reason, high-growth industries are often said to have "superneeds."

To provide benefits for superneeds in high-growth accounts, "superproducts" may have to be sold. A superproduct is not a single product. It is a managed package of related products, services, and systems. Its purpose is not just to offer a larger unit of sale. The main objective of a superproduct is to solve comprehensive problems that can improve customer profits quickly and on a large scale.

Superproducts offer a customer the advantages of one-stop shopping. They offer their supplier the opportunity to become a major partner. At the same time, they shut out competitive invasion of a key account by closing off entry points that would otherwise invite penetration.

## Easing Into Superproducts

What is the easiest way to construct a superproduct? At first, it might seem to be by pairing products that are complementary or supplementary. But products alone, no matter how many are assembled together, do not add up to a superproduct.

It takes service values to make a superproduct. Only services can support most products sufficiently to give them a premium operating advantage. Services are also crucial injustifying superior margins, because they enable fast-growing customers to apply products for maximum operating and financial benefits.

Services that can add the highest values to superproducts run to two types: educational and financial. The contribution of educational services is twofold. One is to help customers extract greater rewards from a superproduct's installation, operation, or maintenance. The second is to teach them how to calculate their improved rewards by computing their newly lowered costs or, more importantly to growth customers, how to put a value on their increased sales revenues.

Financial services such as deferred payments, rental, or leasing can contribute even more fundamentally to premium price. They may make it affordable for a customer to obtain a superproduct and later to upgrade it or replace it. In the prescription of superproducts, the rule of "necessity and sufficiency" can be a useful guide. A superproduct should contain only enough products and services to improve customer profits.

This guideline helps protect you from the twin temptations to underengineer or overengineer a superproduct. If it is overengineered, it will probably have to be overpriced to the point where its return on the customer's investment will be significanlty reduced or nullified. If it is underengineered, its performance inadequacies may contribute to customer dissatisfaction. This can invite competitive inroads. In the interests of avoiding underengineering, one or more of a superproduct's modules or service components may be obtained from other suppliers—even competitors—to round out its ability to deliver benefits.

## Recognizing Common Opportunities for Superproducts

Two major types of opportunities can provide the impetus you need for the creation of superproducts for highgrowth customers:

1. Customer business functions that require frequent servicing, constant monitoring, or sophisticated knowledge to operate and maintain.
2. Advances in your own technology that can produce new customer benefits.

The Dresser-Wayne superproduct is a good example of how both of these opportunities can be combined. It consists of several gas pumps and their monitoring consoles as the nucleus of the superproduct. It also contains a cash management control system, data storage and handling modems, a training program, financing options that include a lease program, and an optional architectural plan to reconstruct individual gas station configurations to maximize their throughput of customers each day. The business functions of this superproduct serves require a high frequency of attention and ongoing monitoring and include sophisticated electronics that take the place of skilled operators.

## SUPERPRODUCTS TO MEET CUSTOMER NEEDS FOR ONGOING SERVICE OR NEW KNOWLEDGE

When a customer's normal use situation requires periodic servicing, replacement parts, consumables, or sophisticated operating knowledge, it is a natural candidate for a superproduct. The superproduct's hardware—its product components—may be a one-time or infrequently updated sale. The servicing it requires and its replacement parts and consumables can generate repeat sales. Over the useful life of the superproduct, repeat sales will account for its major contribution to income.

The repeat sales also provide a second benefit. They assure continuity with your key customers. They offer a valid, profit-making reason for your representatives to return again and again to sell. This gives them the opportunity to seek out new or further needs that can be supplied and upgrade the superproduct installation with more sophisticated hardware and accessories. Many superproducts include elements like these:

- A service agreement to provide recurrent maintanance, repair, and replacement parts and consumables.
- An educational service to teach customers how to use the superproduct. This service may involve an intensive initial teaching program suplemented by periodic refresher courses that are delivered in person or through media.

- A turnkey operational service to provide a core of trained personnel who can act as a surrogate staff in putting the customer's superproduct to work at once.
- A service-fee type of lease to help customers finance their superproducts.

The best type of customers are those who have been educated in a superproduct's capabilities to improve their profit. Educated customers know the full range of benefits to expect and how to achieve them. As a result, they are able to extract the highest profit contribution, because their people have a high level of operating skills. They should also have the greatest incentive to upgrade their original purchase by continually setting new and more ambitious objectives.

A superproduct's educational components must help customers maximize their understanding of its benefits. The need for smart customers is dictated by an essential fact of superproduct life: The "hardware" expense you charge your customers can generally be amortized over time; their personnel costs, however, will probably rise. The majority of dollars spent over a superproduct's life cycle go to pay its operators, not to finance its hard components. From the customers' point of view, education in cost-efficient operation is vital in extracting the full contribution you can make to their profit.

Customer education also helps improve your own profit. By teaching customers the proper operation and maintenance of your superproducts, you are taking out a form of insurance policy against undue repair bills for which you may be liable under contract. You may also be able to avoid or at least defer customer demands for service, which can come at awkward times and cause unplanned costs.

For customers whose operations are governed by compliance legislation, an educational course in conforming to its controls is virtually required. Four other courses may also be included in a customer-education curriculum: operation and maintenance guidelines, profit-improvement evaluation of superproduct performance, forthcoming technological innovations that may affect a customer's operations, and finance options.

There are three basic options for superproduct financing. *Cash flow financing* is designed to pay for a superproduct and optimize your customer's cash flow at the same time. The purchase plan can be geared to a growing customer's income cycle, so that low payments can be made at first, then larger payments, and finally a third-stage drop-off. For businesses affected by seasonal cycles, a deferred or skip-payment schedule can permit smaller payments, or even no payments at all, to be made during low-income periods.

Two other financing methods are a *monthly service fee,* which is payable until the price is paid in full, and *leasing,* which permits a complete schedule of benefits to be enjoyed on a perpetual rental basis.

While these approaches differ, they share three similarities. They permit a growing customer to obtain the added values of a superproduct immediately, without waiting until they can be afforded. A series of relatively small expenditures is substituted in each case for an undigestible big lump. The option also exists for the customer to purchase at any time.

There are additional advantages to the service fee method. Because payment is extended over time, it may enable a customer to hedge against inflation. Another reason to defer payment is the possibility that you will upgrade a superproduct's performance characteristics during the life of the service fee. If this occurs, your customers can benefit at any time from your new technical developments at no additional cost.

Like service-fee financing, leasing is often an alternative to outright purchase for growing customers. Leasing is a form of rental. Under a lease, customers acquire benefits without the cost of possession. They can conserve cash and borrowing power to keep funding their growth. Leasing can be the preferred financing option whenever total dollar cost appears high, but the profit on freed capital can outweigh the cost. Leasing is also a popular option whenever asset ownership is not an advantage, as it may not be in a situation of high growth.

## SUPERPRODUCTS TO MEET CUSTOMER NEEDS FOR NEW TECHNOLOGY

When technology is undergoing rapid or significant change in your industry, the creation of superproducts may confer significant benefits both to you and to your account customers who are themselves growing from innovative technologies.

Many customers will want your new technology. Even those who want it first will be apprehensive, however. They will be beset by four reservations:

1. *Reliability:* Can they depend on it?
2. *Capability:* Will it perform?
3. *Affordability:* Is it cost-effective?
4. *Compatibility:* How does it fit in?

In order to raise their levels of comfort on these issues to the point where they will buy, a superproduct and its added educational and financial values may have to be offered. The superproduct can provide reassurance that questions of reliability and capability have been answered. Its attendant educational and financial values can help ensure affordability together with compatible installation and operation.

Other customers will prefer to wait out the debugging of a new technology. A second type of superproduct can be created to meet their more conservative needs. This can take the form of a hybrid or interim product that will importantly upgrade existing operations but will not threaten their reliability, because it will be highly compatible and more easily affordable.

## Selling Superproducts by Consultation

Superproducts do not reveal their operating and financial advantage by themselves. They require an interpreter who can prove their contribution in advance of purchase. This requires two skills. One is function smartness: Each sales representative must know the costs or revenue-producing ability of the customer functions to be affected. Second, the representative must know how to quantify the dollar values by which they will be affected.

The consultative approach to superproduct sales changes more than just selling style. It also alters the nature of the product benefit, that is, of what is being sold. Superproduct selling removes the emphasis from product performance and places it on the added value of the customer's improved profits.

Of all the components in a superproduct sale, the key account sales representatives can be the greatest adders of value. They scope the customer business function whose profit contribution is to be improved. They calculate the value of a problem and prescribe a solution of greater value. They define the solution in operating and financial terms. Then they structure the superproduct that will deliver the solution, manage its sale, install it, supervise and measure its performance in terms of improving customer profit, and upgrade it over time. In all of these activities, they learn more and more about the customers' business problems. At the same time, the customers learn from them more and more about your solutions. They share together in analyzing problems and measuring solutions; in other words, they consult.

In the same way that they define the superproduct they sell in financial terms rather than physically, the key account sales representatives segment their "customers." Purchasing management remains on its own tier. An upper tier is now accessible, composed of middle and top management. Because key account sales representatives have something to sell at upper levels—profits instead of products, new values instead of added costs, an investment instead of a cost, and a return on investment instead of an expense—their top customer tiers will be open to them.

IBM approaches the top-tier management of its key retail growth customers in a model consultative fashion on behalf of its 3660 superproduct, a computer-assisted checkout station. IBM sales representatives promote the profit-improvement benefits of reduced costs and increased sales. "For a store with gross weekly sales of $140,000, savings are projected at $7,651 a month by faster customer checkout and faster balancing of cash registers." The time required to check out an average order is said to be reduced by almost 30 percent. In addition, IBM sales representatives claim that the elimination of time and cost expenses of correcting checker errors can contribute annual savings of more than $91,000 per store.

If a store is growing, its total savings every year can approach one week's gross sales at the $140,000 level.

The net value of these savings falls directly to the store's bottom line. The essential contribution made by the superproduct is to provide added growth funds that supplement the revenues from sales that can be invested for still further growth. This is the superproduct's purpose, aided and abetted in its implementation by the consultation skills of the key account sales representatives and the customer information on which these skills are based.

# Appendix 2

## *Rebranding Strategy for Key Account Sales of Mature Products*

At the top-tier level of a key account's management, results must be sold. There is no choice. Only results will be bought. Results are easiest to establish with products and services that can produce a demonstrably unique operating and financial result in the customer's business. We call such a product a *brand*. Because a brand can deliver a premium result, a premium price can be demanded in return.

Mature products have usually lost their ability to contribute premium results to a customer. They contribute parity results, benefits similar to those that their competitors can supply. This similarity certifies their status as commodities. Since key account sales depend so heavily on premium results, mature products may have to be *rebranded;* that is, rejuvenated with a brand's capability for providing superior operating and financial benefits.

A commodity may be rebranded in two ways. One is by going back to the drawing board for technological revamping. The other is by marketing renovation. The decision is not either-or. Companies that choose technological change will still have to incorporate marketing strategies alongside their new engineering.

## Making Marketing Changes to Rebrand

There are four principal marketing changes to be made before a rebranding can take place:

    1. *Profit-improvement needs analysis.* You will have to learn customer and industry norms for the business functions you affect. What are the norms for cost of sales, and how does your customer compare? What are profit norms on sales? Is your customer above or below them? What is the norm for collection time on receivables, and how far above the norm is your customer? How much money is the customer leaving on the table as a result every year?

    2. *Profit-improvement contribution analysis.* Either by backtracking on previous applications of your product line to customer business functions or by monitoring the effects of prototype installations, you will have to determine each product's ability to lower a function's cost or raise its sales revenues. This capability will then have to be translated in terms of average profit dollars and average percentage rate of return on investment. These averages will provide ballpark guidelines for the specific values you will have to come up with for each function's improved profit contribution within each customer account.

    3. *Systems protection.* You may have to add value to your product by packaging it into a system that will surround it with complementary products and services that can be sold as a single cost-reducing or sales-

increasing unit. The system's combined price can then be presented as an investment. Its profit-improvement capability can be shown as the return on the investment.

4. *Consultative Selling.* Your key account sales force will have to be trained to sell the system's rate of return to customers—not the product and service system that produces it or the mature product that has been incorporated into the system.

The essential difference between Consultative Selling of a rebranded product or system and the vendor selling of commodity products can be dramatized in this way:

A product-driven commodity sales representative in the chemicals business sells "pounds" to customers by saying, "Our product will solve your formulation problem. It is safe, effective, high in quality, in good supply, and available at competitive prices. We provide free application services to help you ensure the solution."

A consultative representative in the same industry makes a very different approach, even though the product is completely undifferentiated: "Your formulation functions can be reduced in their yearly cost to you by $50,000. In return for a one-time $100,000 investment, you can expect a first-year saving of $50,000 and an annual saving thereafter of $50,000. This gives you payback in two years and adds $50,000 to your profit every year for as long as your formulation process remains the same."

In the first instance, a mature product is being sold on its comparative technical specifications and the performance benefits that can be derived from them. Since competition has matched them, one of two things must happen. Either increasingly finite distinctions must be painstakingly explained by the representative, raising the cost of every sale, or the price must be progressively lowered, reducing the representative's margins.

In the second instance, the customer's investment and the amount and flow of the return it will yield are being used as the basis for a purchase decision. The product remains a commodity. Through rebranding, its benefits it can be sold at a premium price.

## Rebranding One of the World's Largest Companies

In the late 1960s, AT&T was catapulted by legislative fiat from a monopolistic utility into the competitive marketplace. In common with most utilities, AT&T strength had been in providing reactive service, not in campaigning for aggressive sales. Its market knowledge was weak. It knew its customers in terms of their peculiar arrays of wiring installations, but not as businesses with problems that could be solved by the application of telecommunications technology. It was organized along operating lines, not according to end-user markets. Its monopoly position had allowed the company to control the rate of obsolescence for its products and to commercialize new technology as management, not the market, decreed. As a result, the majority of its outstanding hardware was composed of mature products.

Within a short period of time, this mature inventory was in key account competition with IBM, ITT, and GTE as well as with young, dynamic marketers whose technology was responsive to market needs and whose prices were lower. Under this type of pincers attack, AT&T turned to three strategies to preserve, and to grow, the commercial and industrial business sector of its multibillion-dollar annual revenue stream.

1. *Industry-need specialization.* As a utility, AT&T
had segmented its markets according to customer size:
small general businesses or major users. Today, market
segmentation is based on industry needs to use telecommunications technology for reducing operating costs or
for increasing sales revenues. In each segment, AT&T
has come to recognize that its single most important
growth resource is its industry information base on
where customer costs can be reduced and how customer
sales revenues can be improved.

2. *Industry-by-industry positioning.* By applying its
knowledge of industry costs and sales opportunities that
can be affected by telecommunications, AT&T is attempting to gain a position as each industry's preferred
"profit-improving problem solver." The company's
main approach to customers is financial. The problems
for which it prescribes, installs, and monitors solutions
are considered solved only when customer profits have
been improved.

Key account managers and their marketing, technical, and information teams are being taught to carry out
a three-step sales procedure with customers: (1) Identify
a problem and quantify its effect; (2) Quantify the effect
of the most cost-effective system to solve the problem;
(3) Sell the dollars-and-cents effect as representing the
value added by AT&T. A simplified case story will
illustrate the Consultative Selling approach.

A typical problem that can be solved by communications technology is a sluggish accounts receivable
process that deprives a customer of access to cash flow.
In one customer, AT&T discovered that four separate
functions—billing, accounting, sales, and legal—were
involved in past-due collections. Twenty-two separate
steps, each adding costs, were necessary to collect many
receivables. Others were never collected. The average

annual earnings loss on receivables outstanding more than 30 days was $1.75 million. This was the true cost to the customer of the collection system.

To solve the problem, AT&T prescribed a telemarketing collection system. The customer's annual investment is about $350,000. The net annual saving to the customer is $1.4 million, all of which can be brought down to the bottom line as the increased annual profit contributed by AT&T.

3. *Return-on-investment (ROI) sales consultation.* AT&T has taken on the new posture of consulting on the improvement of its customers' profit, not simply supplying customers with hardware and technological know-how. Customers are no longer being asked to spend money, incur costs, or lease equipment. Instead, sales presentations are adopting the style of financial plans that document a positive return on the customers' investment. A system becomes valued by a customer according to the ROI it will deliver, not the cost of the mature products from which it has been assembled.

## Creating a Rebranding Doctrine

Rebranding challenges the law of business gravity that products that descend into maturity can rarely be rejuvenated. This has become unwritten doctrine in many long-established companies. If rebranding is to become a key account sales strategy, it will have to be committed to a written doctrine that will have the force of a sales policy statement.

A rebranding doctrine such as the one shown here can play a powerful teaching and motivating role by its treatment of three key subject areas. One seeks agreement on the purpose of rebranded businesses, so that their contribution to growth profits will be understood and accepted. A second subject explains the premium pricing capability of rebranded products. The third subject fixes an irreplaceable role of key account selling as the prime strategy that educates customers about the nature and dimension of the added value in which they will be asked to invest.

### REBRANDING DOCTRINE

1. The principal objective of key account sales is to grow incremental profits.
2. The principal means of growing incremental profits is to obtain premium price.
3. The basis for premium price is the ability to deliver premium value.
4. A rebranded product's price is based on the value of the customer's return on the investment needed to acquire the added value.
5. The principal capability for rebranding is knowledge of how customer costs can be reduced and how sales can be increased.

Rebranding can move more than products. It moves top-tier selling to the forefront of corporate disciplines. By doing so, it moves companies as suppliers closer to their sources of funds, their customers.

# Appendix 3

## *Market-Centering Strategy for Key Account Sales to Dedicated Markets*

There is no substitute for market dedication as the source of profit growth from sales. Market dedication means focusing resources on specific markets that are the core of your profit contribution. The best way to accomplish this resource focus is to build it into the organizational structure of your business, so that your major markets become the centers around which your key account sales take place.

Companies that adopt top-tier selling as a way of life are increasingly organizing around their key markets instead of around their product or processing capabilities.

IBM has organized its operations according to its key markets, such as institutions like hospitals and retail establishments like supermarkets. Xerox Information Systems Group, which sells copiers and duplicators, has converted from geographical selling to vertical selling by industry. Even the strict technical-processing orientation of some scientific companies is giving way to a combined product and market orientation. In its electronics prod-

uct marketing, Hewlett-Packard has created a sales and
service group that concentrates separately on the electri-
cal manufacturing market, while another group serves
the market for aerospace. Still other groups concentrate
their sales exclusively on the markets for communications or transportation equipment.

General Electric has constructed market-centered
business groups for its major appliance and power-gen-
eration businesses. For GE, the process of reorganizing
from a product to a market orientation has been especially difficult. An average department contained three
and one-half product lines and served more than one
business or, more frequently, only a part of a major
business. Electric motors, for example, were divided
among eight departments. Home refrigerators were split
between two departments, even though the only significant product difference was the way the doors open. In
such a setup, department managers understandably became oriented to specific product lines rather than to the
needs of a total market.

In other companies, a wide range of businesses are
being centered in one fashion or another on their markets. At Mead, broad market clusters serve customer
needs in home building and furnishings, education, and
leisure. Monsanto has organized a Fire Safety Center
that consolidates fire-protection products from every
sector of the company and groups them according to the
market they serve: building and construction, transportation, apparel, or furnishings. Revlon has been engaged
in "breaking up the company into little pieces": Six
autonomous profit centers are each designed to serve a
specific market segment.

PPG Industries has been examining the benefits of
systemizing the sales of its paint, ceramics, and glass

divisions through a Home Environment Center. The center's product mix could look like this:

Interior Protection and Performance Group

- Glass doors
- Ceramic kitchen countertops and work surfaces
- Interior household paints

Exterior Protection and Performance Group

- Glass doors, windows, and window walls
- Ceramic poolside and picnic areas
- Exterior household paints

By making a market the center of a sales organization's focus instead of a product, a process, or a region, banks have been serving the common financial needs of manufacturers of electronics systems with a dedicated key account sales force. Another separate sales force calls on drug and cosmetics accounts. Still another sells financial sources to household product makers.

## Benefits of Market Centering

Defining your business according to your key customer markets by organizing to serve comprehensive sets of their needs with dedicated sales groups can produce several major benefits:

1. A market center forms a natural supply center. The sales and distribution of all the products and services your company makes that can be used by the same market are centralized with a single sales organization.

2. A market center ensures that customers will be required to deal only with its representative to gain access to the sum total of your company's product lines and services.

3. A market center permits the key account sales representatives and their support teams who are dedicated to a single industry to become unusually well versed in knowing its people, problems, and the customer processes into which they must sell your products.

4. A market center provides a ready-made environment for an industry database on its problems and opportunities that you can solve.

5. A market center allows its customers to identify you as a premier source of supply that specializes in solving their unique problems. This creates a predisposed opportunity for you to develop an institute approach to your market by acting as its chief information center and educator as well as marketer.

## Guidelines for Market Centering

If you are currently centering your key account sales operations around one or more product lines, the manufacturing processes that make them, or the geographical territories in which your customers do business, three guidelines will help you to center on your market.

1. A market center must be chartered to serve a market that is defined according to closely related needs. This permits the market to be served by a diversified system of products and services that, taken together, supply a combination of

closely related benefits. The market center may sell two or more related products in a single sale or sell a system composed of products and their related services.

2. Because a market center is operated as a profit center, it should be administered by an industry sales manager. Unlike product managers or brand managers, or even market managers who are merely profit-accountable, industry sales managers are responsible for both profit and volume. They enjoy considerable authority in running their businesses. They command the key decisions. They set prices, control costs, and are charged with operating their market centers for a satisfactory profit on sales.

3. Once a key account sales group is market-centered, its storehouse of market information becomes its key asset. Through market centering, an industry information center can be set up to store and give broad industrywide access to its market knowledge on a fee basis.

Two case histories will illustrate how these guidelines have been implemented by two very different corporations, NCR and General Foods, in order to achieve a similiar objective: to have a single sales representative be able to serve all or most of each key customer's needs in the industry of the representative's dedication.

THE NCR APPROACH

NCR has organized its traditional product-line sales approach into a strategy of "selling by vocation" on an industry-by-industry basis. Each vocation is a broad industry grouping that forms a specific market definable by reasonably cohesive needs. NCR is focusing a separate sales force on each of the following vocational markets: financial institutions, retailers, commercial and industrial businesses, and computer customers in medical, educational, and government offices.

NCR's market-centered sales organization enables the company to be more competitive, especially in the marketing of systems. In each market, the NCR key account sales representative assigned to it can sell coordinated systems of numerical recording and sorting products. Previously, each sales representative could sell only one divisional or departmental product line. As a result, a customer decision maker could be involved with several NCR sales representatives. No one of them could possibly know the sum total of the customer's numerical control needs, let alone be able to serve them. Under the market-centered approach, the same retail industry sales representative who sells an NCR cash register to a department store can also search out and serve the store's needs for NCR accounting machines, data entry terminals, and a mainframe computer. If the representative needs help, he can organize a team with other NCR representatives who can bring the required strength to a proposal. The product groups the representative sells are still manufactured separately. The centralized sales approach is the innovation that makes the difference.

By selling systems of products through a single sales representative or sales team, rather than selling individual products through many uncoordinated representatives, NCR believes it is helping its key customers achieve greater profit improvement. It can prescribe systems that solve comprehensive problems that would otherwise remain immune to single-product solutions. Sales management also believes it can expand its profitable sales volume by selling larger packages and insulating its position against competition.

Each vocational market center's full range of recording and sorting needs is becoming better known to NCR. In turn, by specializing in seeking out and serving these needs, each of NCRs' vocational sales organizations is becoming known for expertise in its market, almost as if it were an independent specialist company. Moreover, every sales group can utilize the total financial and technical resources of the company for professional counsel and support in developing, prescribing, and installing product systems.

## THE GENERAL FOODS APPROACH

Whereas NCR was motivated to center on its market by the increasing preferences of its customers for systems and by the relentless competitive pressures of IBM, General Foods revised its approach because of internal strains and frustrations. In the early 1970s, new product winners either stopped coming out of product development at their former rate or carried an unreasonable cost. Better knowledge of the needs of its consumers was obviously required if the company's product developers were to harmonize their technologies with the new life-styles influencing the demand for processed foods. At the same time, the needs of the company's customers at the retail level required new responses. Competitive brands were proliferating, clamoring for shelf and display space. An increasingly attractive profit on sales was making private-label products more acceptable to the major supermarket chains.

These events combined to place unprecedented strains on the company's divisional structure, which was the legacy of a generations-old policy of acquisition.

General Foods' major food divisions—BirdsEye, Jell-O, Post, and Kool-Aid—had evolved historically, each according to the process technology that it had brought into the company. As the scope of each division's product categories grew, it was inevitable that one division's consumer provinces would be impinged on by other divisions and also that any given market would be served in a fragmented rather than a concentrated manner. Divisional sovereignties frequently made it impossible for the company to dominate a market that was served by two or more divisions with related product categories but with different styles and degrees of commitment.

Often more damaging for new-product development was the way in which division managers respected a no-man's land between their provinces. This left gaps in product categories that gave competitors a clear shot. Even when they missed, the gaps prevented General Foods from establishing a position of undeniable category leadership.

The General Foods approach to market centering has been to reorganize its process-oriented division structure into separate selling organizations. Each market center concentrates on selling families of products made by different processing technologies but consumed by the same market segment. The Dessert Food Center, for example, coordinates the sales strategy for all desserts, whether they are frozen, powdered, or ready-to-eat. The Breakfast Foods center sells breakfast drinks made from three different processing technologies. The Pet Food Center sells dog foods, regardless of whether they come from freeze-dried, dry pellet, or semimoist processes.

Dessert Food Center

- Powdered mixes
- Frozen
- Canned ready-to-eat

Breakfast Food Center

- Powdered beverage mixes
- Frozen
- Canned ready-made

Pet Food Center

- Dry pellet
- Semimoist
- Freeze-dried

This approach of centering entire product families on a market relates the sales organization closely to the needs of the company's retail customers and end-user consumers. Each market center functions like a miniature division. It draws on the full range of corporate technologies and support services such as market research, production and new-product development. Its primary mission is to capture its market by concentrating the corporation's complete range of resources on the market.

## Obtaining Support Services Under Market Centering

Market centering decentralizes the management of key account sales. On the other hand, it centralizes many of the support services that industry sales managers and their key account sales representatives must use. Four groups of service functions are consolidated in many market-centered organizations:

*Development services* combine new-market research and development with new-product R&D under a single director. In this way, the market orientation of

R&D—historically one of the chief stumbling blocks in raising a company's level of responsiveness to its customers—is accomplished organizationally. New-market needs, new-process technology, and new-product development are able to interact harmoniously rather than competitively. With market centering, the traditional vice-presidential functions for marketing and R&D can be subsumed under the director of development's functions.

*Control services* take on the basic research to evaluate the effectiveness of established product and service-system marketing. They also provide the necessary recruitment, compensation and motivation, training and development, legal, and financial functions.

*Production services* coordinate engineering and manufacturing operations.

*Promotion services* combine sales, advertising, and publicity.

## Two-Way Growth Opportunity

Market centering may come to rank in importance with Alfred Sloan's decentralization of General Motors along market-segmented lines. Market-centered companies see themselves regaining a customer focus that often became blurred by Proctor & Gamble's brand management system. While contemporary with Sloan's market awareness, brand management directed the styles of many corporate formats away from customers and back to products. When product and brand management were imposed on the traditional manufacturing division and on the pyramid type of organization, which was adapted for the needs of commercial business from Von Moltke's general staff concept, progress toward market centering slowed for half a century.

In the mid-1960s, the beginning of a new thrust toward the customer was signaled by the advent of free-form marketing groups. They were allowed to cut across corporate pyramids whenever unusual market sensitivity was demanded in an operation. A variety of problem-solving task forces and project management teams came into being for much the same reason; they represented jerry-built improvisations to defeat a product-oriented or process-centered organizational system.

Market centering a business can give it a two-way flexibility. Each of its major markets can be sold to more intensively once it is established as the center of a business. The same market can be sold to more exten-sively as well. Its related needs can be sought out and served along with the primary needs you are already meeting. This will provide you with a two-lane avenue for accelerated sales growth.

# Index